$14.00

# BACKPACKING for TROUT

*Distributed by*
*The Stephen Greene Press*
*Box 1000*
*Brattleboro, VT 05301*

# BACKPACKING for TROUT

### Written and Illustrated by
# BILL CAIRNS

## Introduction by
## "Lefty" Kreh

Stone Wall Press, Inc.
1241 30th Street, NW
Washington, D.C. 20007

Library of Congress Cataloging in Publication No. 80-51956

ISBN 0-913276-32-4

Cover design by Kathy Jungjohann
Cover photo by the author

52,319

Published September 1980

# CONTENTS

# INTRODUCTION

Backpacking offers challenges, both physical and mental, and opportunities and rewards. If you're a trout fisherman, those rewards are even greater. The backpacker gets into country or parts of watersheds rarely visited by the lazier angler. The fish are wilder and bigger, and the solitude enhancing the magnificent scenery is certainly worth lugging your camping gear and fishing tackle to.

This book offers much practical information about all phases of camping. One useful item derived from the author's many hours at the sport, is the check-list that will guide you in assembling the gear you need. How to get maps, both of this country and Canada, and how to use them, is very well treated, and important information on selecting the proper equipment is included. Especially useful is the chapter that deals with backpacks.

Aside from all of the valuable information on camping, the author tells you how to combine camping with trout fishing. One good, basic, understandable chapter deals with the foods that trout feed on, and how this information and subsequent observations will help you catch more trout. Another well-done chapter tells how to select correct fly and spinning tackle, and what lures to use with each. How to fish ponds, streams, and lakes (they're all different) suddenly becomes understandable.

If you enjoy fishing and walking, you'll discover that you will be carrying this book in your pack.

Lefty Kreh

# The Starting Point

## Uniting Backpacking and Trout Fishing

Backpacking and trout fishing. For some they have been long term parallel passions. For others, one interest has evolved from participation in the other. The experiences of two friends typify these evolutions. The first, an experienced backpacker, explained how he became interested in trout fishing. One late afternoon he made his camp near a small, remote mountain pond. After an early evening meal when the clean-up chores were completed, he walked along the shoreline and out onto a rocky point that jutted well into the pond. Settling down, he was soon absorbed in solitude. The gentle, day breezes had stilled, and pond-bordering trees lost their images to the stillness of reflection. A widening circle marred and distorted one mirrored image. Then more circles, each quietly forming, widening and dissipating. The pond stirred with rising trout moving in apparent unison to newly emerging mayflies. Just a few yards off the rocky point he saw the polished flank of a heavy trout as it rolled and was captured briefly in the last slanting rays of sunlight. Fascinated, he stayed there long after the last light. From these moments, spent quietly and alone, he resolved to learn about trout fishing. Now, several years later, he plans most of his backpacking trips around remote fishing possibilities.

Or, the angler. We met first on a Wyoming trout stream and then again on a return flight east from Denver. There he told me of his own transition from angler to backpacking angler.

It began on a warm spring day bursting with the promise of mayflies and rising trout. He had waded to a spot, familiar from past experience, where it was an easy cast to the brown trout that would soon station himself by a fallen log. Above him the current flowed in a gentle, bank-hugging diversion that curled to follow the contour of the intrusive log. The delicate mayflies sailed that current, oblivious to the trout and the birds about to feed on their numbers. The brown trout would certainly be by the end of the log, just as he always was when out in a feeding posture. Overhead the cedar waxwings were already nervously alert in streamside trees. Some hopped quickly from branch to branch, others darted out in brief, aborted flights in their own anticipation of the hatch.

A single mayfly popped to the surface, drifted with the slick current, and took to tentative wings. More mayflies followed. The angler took it all in and his eyes darted back to the feeding station. Indeed, the brown trout had appeared, having ghosted from his resting place to take a feeding attitude. He watched the trout examine, drift back, and finally tilt up easily to accept the stream-bred fare. Casually powerful thrusts then returned the trout to his original lie. The angler noted the feeding rhythm and became attuned to it. He set the rod in motion. Lengthening pulls extended the pale fly line and the leader unrolled to set the delicate imitation in the established drift line. The trout came quickly with misplaced confidence. Moments later the angler was at mid-stream, bending to admire and then release his catch.

A cobweb fell across his neck. Reaching casually to brush it away, he became aware of another presence. Another fisherman had watched and now, unbelievably, had intruded. A spinning lure was cast directly over the angler's head. The "cobweb" was trailing monofilament.

The angler waded ashore to confront the newcomer. Soon his anger dissipated to a peculiar mixture of sadness and resignation. The intruder was fishing for the first time and knew nothing of time-honored rituals of stream courtesy. He simply reacted when he saw a fine trout taken, and wanted desperately to do the same. My friend soon left, feeling somehow saddened and betrayed, for he found the intruder to be a likeable sort and eager to learn. Down deep my friend would have preferred confrontation. Then he would have spoken his mind, unleashed his indignations and left, if still angry, at least partially compensated by the venting of those indignations.

On the drive home he thought of the changes he had witnessed to his favorite streams and of the increasing pressures they were being asked to absorb and endure. Then he recalled a conversation he'd had a year earlier with a warden supervisor in northern New England. The warden told him of remote ponds, rarely visited, that lay a day's hike in from the road. There brook trout to three pounds were still a possibility. He also recalled walking far upstream on a Pennsylvania river—beyond the influence of the casual, roadside angler. He found both trout and solitude that day.

From tentative, experimental day trips, backpacking for a weekend or a week was the natural progression. Through backpack angling he found his solution to overcrowded streams. This angler continues to fish the nearby civilized waters, but each season he makes time to backpack into remote spots that lie away from the influence of the roadside hordes.

4

No matter how they come together, there is a natural affinity between backpacking and trout fishing. Despite many varied encroachments on our remaining wild places, there are still havens of quiet grandeur and delight where senses, jaded by the cacophony of modern life, reawaken and revitalize. There is not the wilderness there once was, but enough still remains to captivate and charm those who come to it with respect, concern, common sense and the willingness to accept it on its own terms.

This book is written for those backpackers desirous of learning the fundamentals of trout fishing and for those anglers who would like to drop a line on quieter, more productive streams. This is by no means the last word on either subject. It is the starting point to the natural union of two, separate pleasures, each enhanced by the other.

*Bordered by wildflowers, this remote stream gives up a husky trout and contributes to a memorable "total experience."*

# 2.

# THE SHAKEDOWN TRIP

Backpacking is relatively safe and can be learned in easily progressive stages. True, the wilderness has killed the unprepared, but when a modicum of common sense regarding weather, clothing selection, health, and site selection is combined with sensible equipment selection and proper use, the woods unquestionably are safer than the highways. Backpacking is also relatively simple. Simple, by the way, is not synonomous with easy. There is very definite physical involvement. Your feet are the wilderness wheels, as it were. Combined with your legs, heart and lungs, they provide the drive, wind, and stamina essential to a pleasurable experience.

The first considerations are adequate footgear and general physical preparation. The standard criteria for footwear are adequate support, traction, protection, and comfort. Ultimately you will see everything from sneakers to combat boots along the trails, but a lightweight pair of hiking boots are the best choice. Lacking these, you might consider the so-called work boots. Moderately priced, they provide fair support and adequate traction on most beginning landscapes. For the first short shakedown trip or two they should be adequate. However, if you are at all serious about taking up backpacking, the first equipment decision that must be made is the hiking boot. When you purchase boots, begin an immediate, gradual routine of breaking them in and don't take seriously to the trail until they are well broken in.

Beyond adequate footwear, the other half of our initial equation is general physical conditioning. These conditioning aspects are slightly elusive, for backpacking is for everyone with no age or sex barriers. The usual concern is not physical strength *per se*, but adequate wind and stamina. If your life has been largely sedentary lately, some pretrail preparation is advisable. There are several, helpful recreational activities: walking, day hiking, jogging, swim-

*Day packs are always useful to the angler/packer and are available in a wide variety of sizes and styles. The Kelty Swallow (pictured) is a full panel opening model with a large, undivided compartment.*

ming, cyclying, tennis or other racquet or court games. Okay, you've scanned the list and find you: a) dislike jogging, b) can't swim, c) don't own a bicycle, and, d) can't get court time. All is not lost. Just plan on walking and day hiking as often as possible. Indeed, many experienced hikers feel the best preparation is simply to load a pack with about fifteen to twenty pounds and get out and walk the nearby countryside as often as possible. This approach is a good one and parallels can be found in some other activities that require a lot of walking. One close friend devotes much of his time in the fall to upland game bird hunting in the crazy quilt landscape of Vermont. He's found no other preseason program quite as effective as simply going out and walking the covers, slogging along the lowland gullies, straddling the old stone walls and climbing the hills in gunless simulation of what he'll be doing in forthcoming weeks.

The would-be backpacker can start a similar routine. Get a simple, well made day bag. Most of the moderately sized models are capable of holding up to about twenty pounds. Start a routine of regular day hikes as often as your schedule permits. Perhaps there is a stream you know that works far away from the road; possibly a hilltop pond is an easy two or three miles off the highway with a good trail leading to it. Maybe it's just grabbing the camera, a couple of extra lenses, and going out and tramping the countryside. Even on these rather benign conditioning trips, it is advisable to carry certain items. A classic necessity list was first advanced by the Seattle Mountaineers. It recognizes that you should, at all times, be prepared for the unforeseen. It recommends extra food, extra clothing, matches, firestarter, first aid kit, light (either flash light or headlamp), sun glasses, knife, topographic map and compass. Since the list was first advanced several authorities have come forth to suggest possible additions that would supplement the essentials nicely without taking up excessive room. Consider, for example, taking a large three or four mil plastic sheet, tarp or space blanket as possible emergency shelter. Then, fifty feet of $\frac{1}{16}$ or $\frac{1}{8}$ inch cord. This has multiple uses besides rigging an emergency shelter. Change for an emergency phone call and some signaling device could also come in handy.

I've never paid the attention to this I perhaps should have, but one student in a fishing class I was involved with told of breaking an ankle. His shouting could not be heard above the rush of water, but the whistle he had tucked away in his vest did bring attention from his downstream companions. Another possibility might be a metal mirror. Three of anything is a universal distress signal. In season, don't forget insect repellent. Toilet paper is self-explanatory. Pencil and notebook could be handy if a note must be left someplace. If the weather is hot and bright enough to justify wearing sunglasses, you might want a light cap, chapstick and suncream.

Check these items over. None of them is excessively heavy, nor do they take up much space. Knowing you always have them with you is quite comforting. Incidentally, these local day trips are the ideal time to become familiar with the map and compass. You know the landscape and you can learn to relate it to the map in a no-pressure situation. Also, an ankle can be sprained or a knee twisted just as easily two miles from home as it can twenty miles back in the boonies.

All in all, there is ample justification for carrying an "emergency kit" at all times.

Day trips are pleasurable in themselves, and functional in that they are working you towards true trail shape. And that day bag—well, it will continue to be useful. When you've gained some experience and confidence you can strap a sleeping bag to it and use it for solo, go-light, overnight sessions. It can also go along in your regular pack for those times when you plan to establish a main base camp and work out of it in daytime splinter travels.

When you feel you are well prepared for that first overnight or weekend jaunt, there are several options. Ideally you'll have a companion in mind who is already into backpacking. Some major items like stoves and tents are shared. Other items like packs and sleeping bags may be borrowed or rented. This is the best initial approach. Tents, stoves, packs, and sleeping bags are available in any number of competing models, styles and price ranges. It takes a bit of time to sort them out. You can gain time and experience by renting or borrowing for a while, and you can evaluate the equipment in relation to your developing interests, attitudes and intended uses. Costs of equipment continue to escalate. This is further justification for taking your time and making sound selections based on realistic, practical appraisals of your requirements. In addition to the major items of tent, stove, pack, and sleeping bag, your clothing is very important. With the help of your experienced companion, review the clothing you intend to take. Experienced hikers place emphasis on layering clothing to stay warm and dry. Everything you initially need is probably already available in your closets and drawers.

Lacking an experienced companion, there are several ways to contact individuals of similar interest. Check with local tackle shops and backpacking shops. They know the area individuals who are heavily involved. The gear shops can also recommend various local, state, or regional hiking clubs or trail organizations. Many of these organizations conduct regular outings. Although some folks dislike such organizations, they unquestionably serve a valid function for others. Participation in such an outing is an opportunity to associate with and learn from experienced hikers in a well-planned situation.

However, we'll operate on the premise that you have a willing, experienced companion. Through the combination of sharing, borrowing and renting, you are adequately prepared for an easy shakedown weekend. It's time to get together and do the basic planning. How much time will you allot to travel? What is the trail distance and difficulty? How long is the trip planned for? In all probability you'll arrive at easy solutions to these questions. The trip may center around the expected good fishing at some relatively nearby stream or pond. It may center around some nearby slice of semiwild country, an area that is not very difficult but is pleasant with well-marked and maintained trails ideally suited to a weekend shakedown trip. If you get stuck for a destination, there are several information sources you can call on for assistance. Inquiries at tackle shops and gear shops will gather a lot of useful location information. Then check for any nearby National Park Service office, U.S. Forest Service office, Federal Fish and Wildlife Agency, or Bureau of Land Management office. Also, look into your own state agencies that are involved with fishing or park management. Do you know any other fishermen or hikers around town that might have good suggestions to make? Look for information from members of the local rod and gun clubs, members of the local or area hiking or trail organizations. Check the bookstores for canoe guides and area or regional guides. Game wardens are another possible source of helpful information. When you get right down to it, there are any number of knowledgeable sources for trip planning wherever you are located.

Very likely the area planned for your first shakedown will be covered in a guidebook. Books should provide plenty of useful information: distances, average trail times between various points, relative ease of the trails, elevations, and any special attractions such as well-hidden waterfalls or spectacular viewing vistas that you might not otherwise be aware of. Some tend to be so complete that your hear occasional complaints that the joy of self-discovery is gone from any area covered by a guidebook. Perhaps in time you'll even share this viewpoint, but right now that book, combined with the appropriate topo maps, is confidence and knowledge building.

Next, are there any visitor or fire permits required where you plan to travel? If so, can they be obtained by mail or do they require personal pickup? In-person pickup requirements affect your travel arrangements. You want to allow time to get to the agency in question, obtain the permits, travel to trailhead and walk to your first planned overnight with an arrival time well before sundown.

For your first trip, don't try to travel a great deal of distance. Long distance travel usually isn't necessary. Recent energy and gasoline problems appear to be here to stay. One way to contend with them is to get to know your own area better. Any number of fine opportunities may exist within easy striking distance that you've previously overlooked. One individual suggested a method that focuses attention on the relatively local opportunities. Pick up a standard road map of your state or region, figure the fuel tank capacity of your car and the approximate mileage you get from it. Then with pencil and compas draw two circles. Using your home town as the base, the first circle represents distances approximately a half tank of gas away; the second circle represents full tank of gas away. Obviously the distances will vary with the car you own. Let's say the first circle represents a 150 mile radius of your home, the large one a 300 mile radius. There are bound to be outdoor opportunities in that smaller circle that you have heard about, but just haven't gotten around to yet. The same for the larger circle.

With your destination in mind, check the appropriate topographic maps, any agency maps, and the guidebooks. You may want to plan your travel so that you go in on one trail and out on another. Look for trail possibilities that work around in such a way that you can come out not too far from your original starting point. Or, if the entrance exits are quite far apart, plan on setting up a car shuttle. Leave one car at the entry point, the second car at the planned exit point.

Although the car is the basic transport mode to trailhead, it may be possible to utilize public transportation. We're located about four miles from the Appalachian Trail. It seems that each bus that arrives in town from late spring through fall brings with it a quota of hikers and their gear.

When travel plans are completed, a copy of your intentions should be made and discussed with family or friends. This copy remains with them. It should indicate where you are going, which routes and trails you will be taking, whom you are going with (and their phone number), expected time of return, and the name and phone number of the appropriate agency on whose lands you will be traveling. If there is any chance you will extend the trip another day or so, this should be indicated so family or friends won't take any action until the ultimate deadline is passed by a day or two, or whatever you have agreed on. If possible, leave duplicate maps of your planned itinerary.

In this early shakedown trip, the weight of the pack you carry should not be excessive. Fundamentally, comfort, success, and convenience depend on what is carried. When you are properly equipped the trip is relatively easy. Too little equipment could place you in possible danger; too much equipment is unnecessary and backbreakingly heavy. The elusive "they" say you can carry up to one third of your body weight. Indeed you can, but pack weights approaching this range imply a much longer, more strenuous venture. You should be able to come up with a pack weight about one fifth of your body weight for this weekend trip.

Normally you drive to the trailhead and leave your vehicle locked, taking your keys and wallet with you. In a few areas there have been reports of damage or theft to vehicles so left. You might look into the possibility of leaving your car in town, arriving at the trail via taxi, bus, or having a friend drive you. If these latter options don't exist leave the car and keep the faith.

At trailhead you will do the final pack fitting and adjusting. Some of this may have already been done at home, but virtually everyone seems to field fit the pack and check for proper weight distribution at this point when they are dressed for trail conditions. There may be a trail register. Take a moment to sign in before starting out.

The amount of distance you can cover varies tremendously with the terrain. Your maps and guidebooks have combined to give you a good idea of "average" times for the anticipated distances and your timetable is probably geared pretty much to their advice. On a full daily basis, one of the rules of thumb indicates allowing an average of two hours for each three miles of trail with another hour allotted for each one thousand feet of elevation gained. Thus, ten miles a day is certainly possible. Many will rather routinely do more, many less. The established trail pace should be comfortable, neither too fast or too slow. One potential measure of pace is normal conversation. If you find it difficult to maintain a normal conversation, the pace is getting a bit quick. Rest breaks are somewhat trail dependent. If the going is tough, several short stops are preferred over a single long stop. On a moderate trail a short break about each hour seems appropriate.

At those places where the trail steepens, there are two basic approaches. A few hikers attack, quickening their pace in short, energetic bursts. Then they pause to recover. Then they resume their energetic burst. Most hikers seem to work out a rest step. Pause briefly with each new step just at that time when the lead foot is planted but hasn't yet received body weight. This break in each stride allows a brief, second or more respite with each step taken, and is very helpful with a steep pitch and a heavy pack.

It's ridiculous to advise anyone on how to walk. Still, first timers may not pay enough attention to the trail itself. There are roots, rocks, and occasional obstacles, so keep a good eye on the trail. Also, those adjustments on your pack are functional and you may want to vary them from time to time. You probably will start out with the hip belt tightly taken up. After being on the trail awhile you may want to loosen it somewhat and tighten the shoulder straps. This will effectively shift the load and such an alternating routine helps most hikers. When you come to a stream crossing, unbuckle the hip belt totally. A face down fall with a loaded pack is potentially dangerous. Incidentally, some hikers change to sneakers in stream crossings. In a large group, they may throw the sneakers back and forth until everyone is across. The characters I know just wade on through, change later to dry socks, hang the wet ones on the outside of the pack to dry and walk the boots dry.

When a trail starts to switchback, it is to allow the hiker to make the required elevation gain without working excessively hard. Although there is no temptation to shortcut it going up hill, there may be one when coming downhill. Don't do it! It is destructive and quickly causes erosion. Always stick with the trail. On most trails you will walk single file. Stay with the middle of the trail and don't travel its outer edges. Any rules about trail rights with oncoming parties are informal, based mostly on common sense and normal courtesy. If two parties meet, the one coming down hill should have the right of way. It's easier for those going up to step aside and let them pass. When parties of different sizes meet, the smaller group can more easily step aside and let the larger group pass. Sometimes in the West you will meet horseback groups. These animals usually have very stable temperaments. However, it's best for everyone concerned if the hiker will move to the uphill side of the trail and remain in full view. As the riders pass, speak your greetings rather than waving. A startled horse is trouble—for someone.

On this first shakedown trip you have worked out a good travel plan with an anticipated overnight stop that you will reach well before sundown. This allows plenty of time for setting up camp, meal preparation, clean-up chores, and there is time left for the evening rise or just sitting around and discussing the events of this first day on the trail.

The next morning is your first on the trail You awake and it's refreshingly chilly. Don enough clothes for comfort through the breakfast preparation. If you will be hitting the trail again, it's a good idea to start out dressed so that you are just slightly chilly. You will warm up soon enough. Zipper or button-

12

front, layered clothing helps in heat regulation at these times. As you walk you may notice a "hot spot" forming. Don't wait. Stop! Get the boot and socks off, take a look and repair the problem.

If your plans are to remain in this camp for the day, splitting up to take advantage of the stream fishing nearby, reach for your day pack, include your lunch and the list of essentials, and prearrange with your companion the time and meeting place—probably back at this main site. Then you can wander off downstream to enjoy the angling while your companion heads upstream for the same.

Too soon the weekend is over. But, you've gotten through it and enjoyed every minute of it. You feel weary, but not excessively so. You have a few questions to discuss on the way home with your companion, but overall you now have an idea of the physical effort involved, how physically prepared you are, and you may even be getting a few fixed ideas on equipment selection as you decide the sport definitely is for you. Still, a cautioning note: There is a multiplicity of gear and one short trip isn't enough time to make most of the hard equipment decisions. Why not plan on renting once more? If you carried a traditional frame pack this time, why not try a soft pack next time? Meanwhile, you can be gathering more information from the gear stores and catalogs to supplement your expanding experience.

Make a mental review of the trip. Is there any clothing or other equipment you wished you had along? Are there items you carried but did not use? Were they practical items such as rain gear that just wasn't needed because of continuing good weather, or were they items that you now realize will always be excess baggage? When you start this semicritical review, you are, whether you know it or not, about to become another trail regular—another backpacker. Welcome!

# 3.

# THE INEVITABLE LIST

The overall success of any trip will depend to a large degree on those numerous and varied items carried in your pack. Your potential needs must be adequately anticipated and appropriate equipment selected to meet these needs. Fortunately there are logical separations which will help you plan in a reasonably forthright manner. You require clothing for comfort, heat regulation, and weather protection. You require sleeping comfort, shelter, food and water. You require directional assistance. You need a variety of personal health and first aid items as well as miscellaneous items for equipment maintenance and repair. When these needs are adequately met, then you can look to any extras that catch your eye as fun to have, that add more convenience, or that just add an extra, personalized touch which you can only justify "because you like it."

I would be among the very first to acknowledge the tedium of any equipment list. In justification, there must be a starting point for decision making. You simply cannot send a check for $12,500.00 to R.E.I. or E.M.S. and ask for one each of everything they catalog, though quite possibly each would be happy to hear from you on that basis. In evaluating any list, realize that its interpretation and modification should correspond with your intentions and your seasonal/regional requirements. A dry weather Sierra hiker may be able to place more emphasis on light-weight gear and be generally less concerned with wet trails and damp, humid climates than some others. Those in the Northwest, upper Midwest and here in the Northeast may place less emphasis on going light from a standpoint of pack weight. We, for example, have four and a half seasons to contend with: a day of spring (last year it was on a glorious Wednesday), two months of mud, followed by summer, fall and winter. Overall we have to contend with more damp woods, higher humidity and rainfall totals than dry-country hikers. Wool and synthetics often replace down for their warmth-when-wet capabilities.

Because any listing is rather elastic, the best way to handle it is to be critical of each item: Do I have this, do I need this, do I want this? Get the important stuff in order first. Then and only then can you play games with all the goodies that may have caught your eye. Further, after each of the first few trips, empty out the pack and size up each item. Did I have use for this? Would I need it in an emergency situation? Is this taking up room and weight better allotted to something else? You will soon have a basic set of gear that you know intimately. From that point on the pack will probably always be about half packed and ready to go on short notice. You will quickly be able to make the seasonal modifications for the cooler weather of spring and fall or the warmer summer trips.

# EQUIPMENT LIST

## ITEMS WORN OR OTHERWISE CARRIED ON YOUR PERSON

*Underwear—to suit yourself and existing weather conditions. Avoid nylon as
    being too hot.*
*Hiking shorts or long pants*
*Hiking boots*
*2 Pair Socks—1 light inner and 1 heavier outer pair*
*Sunglasses*
*Hat*
*Pocket knife—and/or small folding belt knife*
*Shirt—short sleeve or long sleeve to suit weather*
*Bandanna*
*Trail snack*
*Wrist watch—if desired*
*(Avoid wearing a large, heavy belt. It can interfere with the hip belt of your
    pack. Choose a soft belt or consider suspenders.)*

## PACKED CLOTHING

*Pack style rain poncho*
*Rain chaps or rain pants*
*Gaiters*
*Extra bandanna or two*
*Extra socks—both light and heavy*
*Extra underwear—or heavier type for cold weather*
*Long pants—(if not worn at start of trip) wool if wet warmth will be
    needed*

*Warm cap*

*Gloves or mittens*

*Wool or otherwise appropriate shirt—with wool shirt, possibly a water-proof shell garment*

*Sweater—consider button or zipper front for better heat regulation*

*Insulated vest or jacket—down or synthetic filled*

*Nylon wind shirt*

## SLEEPING CONSIDERATIONS

*Tarp*

*Tent and fly*

*Groundsheet*

*Sleeping Bag*

*Sleeping pad or air mattress*

*Pillow—stuff clothing in a stuff bag or choose inflatable style*

## KITCHEN

*Stove and windscreen*

*Cookset or two pots, fry pan, (with frypan you may want a light spatula), potgripper*

*Spare fuel in appropriate container*

*Eyedropper and funnel for priming and pouring*

*Cup or bowl to eat from*

*Spoon, knife and fork—'til you lose them*

*Sierra cup*

*G.I. can opener (if you like sardines along trail and don't have opener on your knife)*

*Canteen or baby bottle for water or other liquids*

*Collapsible water carrier*

*Biodegradable soap*

*Nylon scrub pad*

*If using fire—backpacker grill (or bring cheap, light cake rack substitute)*

*Sven saw (or other collapsible saw for cutting larger pieces of down and dead wood)*

*Herbs, spices etc.—carried in 35mm film cans or ziploc bags*

*Adequate food supply packed in individual meal bags*

*(If trip has possibility of being extended a day or two have an adequate supply of food and stove fuel)*

*Reserve or emergency food supply*

*Trail snacks of your choice*

*Aluminum foil*

# PERSONAL—CONVENIENCE—
# HEALTH—DIRECTIONAL

*Water purification tablets*
*Matches—with spare waterproof/windproof matches located variously in your pack*
*Flashlight—spare batteries/bulb*
*Candle—fire ribbon or heat tabs*
*Toilet—razor, liquid hand soap, toothbrush, paste, towel (or your bandanna)*
*Foot powder*
*First aid kit—start with commercial kit. Include booklet, any personal prescription items needed, anti-diarrhetic; then, check with doctor for antibiotic and a heavy duty painkiller which will require a prescription.*
*Snake bite kit (depending where you are going)*
*Insect repellent*
*Whistle, signal mirror, change for emergency phone call*
*Chapstick, suncream, maybe spare sunglasses*
*Spare boot laces*
*Nylon cord 50 to 100 ft.*
*Space blanket or plastic sheet emergency shelter*
*Trowel—for cat hole sanitation*
*Toilet paper*
*Pencil and notepad*
*Camp shoes—booties, moccasins, low cut sneakers*
*Topo (and agency) maps, compass, area guidebook*
*Repair and maintenance kit—consider repair tape, seam sealer, sewing materials, safety pins, pack parts, stove parts, 5 minute epoxy, small screwdriver, mini-pliers, rubber bands, magnifying glass (may help in splinter removal or insect identification when fishing*
*Miscellaneous stuff bags to separate gear*
*Extra plastic bags for leftovers and garbage, etc.*
*Stout container for bear bagging, if needed*

Then there are several possible additions: a belt bag or fanny pack for hobby items such as a camera, film, meter, filters; guidebooks to geology, plants, trees, birds etc.; a day bag for splinter travel when establishing a base camp and radiating out in various day travels; a folding candle lantern may substitute for a fireplace; mini-binoculars; a thermomenter, barometer or altimeter.

The last item I'll mention is a hammock. It's one of those look-good-but-do-I-want-it kind of items. Enter Tony Atwill and a trip to the Adirondacks. We had to walk the last part in the rain. We finally stopped and suspended a tarp. I sat on a piece of plastic over a big, soggy log and watched the ants climb my boots. Tony dug deep into his pack, came out with this hammock, and strung it between two trees. Damn, but he looked obscenely comfortable!

*Local gear shops can provide the personalized service and assistance in fitting which is often required in gear selection. Here, Peter Kavouksorian of Mountain Travelers in Rutland, Vermont, assists in frame pack selection. Most backpacking items are also available by direct mail from the makers, and their catalogs are valuable sources of information.*

Back in the car: When you come off the trail you may want an extra set of dry clothing and extra food for the trip home. Liquor on the trail? Exercise your own judgment.

Agreed, the list looks long. Remember that much of it is made up of small items. Some of the list may be non-essential for you or there may be additions you would make. In any case, it does give you a starting point. Remember that in a group some items are community gear and may not require duplication by everyone. In a family outing dad can carry the tent, stove and cookset. The wife's pack and the childrens' packs can be correspondingly lighter. Also realize that as food and fuel are used along the course of the travel, the packs become progressively lighter.

18

The problems of equipment always continue. Items ultimately wear out and require replacement. New items, heavily advertised and quite eye catching, are regularly introduced. Each backpacker must decide for himself, but the down and dirty advice: To hell with fashion! Worry about function, reliability and durability. Then, if you like the looks, so much the better. Fortunately outdoor gear does tend to be well made, possibly because many of the gear companies are still comparatively small and their personnel are outdoors people themselves. I know I have more faith in my outdoor gear than I do in the conglomerate that produced our last two toaster ovens, seemingly manufactured with a built-in, self-destruct timing element to go off two days after the warranty ran out. The underlying point is not to give in and become obsessed with equipment. Select carefully, but don't be overly concerned about the latest gimmick. Your legs, your back, and your sweat, combined with appropriate, well-designed equipment suited to your needs, are what make (or break) your trip.

# 4.

# THE BACKPACK

The modern pack has opened wide the doors to the wilderness and made it possible for us to range widely in self-contained convenience. These doors have always been slightly ajar as earlier outdoorsmen slipped through, wrestling their gear into the wilderness by means of various pack baskets and pack boards. However, none of these earlier load carrying alternatives were particularly comfortable for trail travel. It was not until after World War II that the wobbly foundations of popular backpacking began to solidify. The innovative advance was the use of a waist strap. This new hip suspension system effectively relieved the neck and shoulder stresses of the Trapper Nelson packboards and made it considerably easier to support and transport heavy loads. Aluminum tubing soon replaced the old style wooden frames. For all practical purposes, the concrete in the modern backpacking foundation was hardening in place to provide support for an embryonic growth industry. As an indication of what has taken place in a relatively short time, Dick Kelty sold twenty-nine handmade packs in 1952. Less than thirty years later the burgeoning industry probably sells in excess of two million packs a year.

I still recommend your first purchase to be a simple day pack. It is ideal for day hikes, and many of these packs are quite suitable for go-light overnight sessions when a sleeping bag is strapped in place. Also, a day pack can be handy item in any main pack when a base camp is to be established and plans are to radiate out in a series of day travels, returning each night to the main camp. The day pack selection is not complex, although it's true there are any number of competing models. They are available in various capacities or sizes and often feature such items as a carrying-hauling loop, ice axe loop, various accessory patches, shoulder straps, and waist bands. Some are compartmented; some are

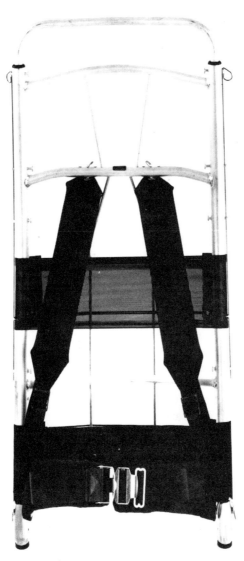

*Perhaps more than anything else the modern pack frame has been responsible for the vast increase in backpacking popularity by relieving the neck and shoulder stresses associated with older style packboards. The modern frame is light, comfortable, durable, and combines with a hip belt suspension system to make load carrying easier. Pictured: the Kelty Massif frame.*

not. There are even a few that are convertible by featuring a zip-out interior divider which allows you to have it either way. Handy and useful as they are, they are not the answer for the go-anywhere, self-contained travel for which a standard-sized backpack is required.

The trail travel standard is the external frame pack. Thoroughly proven after millions of user miles, they are fairly simple, although almost endless variations of the concept are available. Since we are treading a rather fundamental path, my advice is to get the basics in good order before considering gimmicky arrangements that may be more trouble than they're worth. The chosen pack should be fairly light and tough with an adequate capacity to suit your intentions. There should be an adequate number of outside pockets, loops, and patches for the extra gear. Zippers should be durable and reliable as should all closures.

There are three main parts: the frame, the packbag, and the suspension system. The frame may be aluminum, a magnesium alloy, or a molded plastic such as polypropylene. If the original quality is good and the material substantial enough, each of these alternatives have proven themselves in the field. Most frames are rigid. A few are designed to flex somewhat when walking. Frames are available in different lengths to properly match the torso length from shoulder to waist as this will be a critical factor in the proper fit. Some adjustable frame models are well suited for different wearers or growing family members.

There are various frame shapes. The most common version provides a double "S" curved frame to follow the approximate shape of the spine. The time spent assuring a proper fit is well used. The sales person will help select the correct frame length for that important shoulder-to-waist area. Most stores will have sandbags or other weights to simulate a trail load. Load the pack with twenty-five to thirty pounds and try it on. Tighten the hip belt. It should bring most of the weight to your waist. Then adjust the firmly padded shoulder straps for a comfortably firm fit. Walk around for a few moments. Check that the hip belt is comfortable and shows no inclination to slip up or down. Similarly, check the shoulder straps that they don't slip. The backbands are comfort and ventilation aids that keep the pack away from your back while helping to distribute the pack weight properly.

Pack bags attach to the frame in various ways, although a clevis pin and ring arrangement is most common. The bags themselves may be either divided or undivided. Individual preference dictates choice. Some hikers like to separate various items in color-coded stuff bags or plastic bags and stow everything into one main compartment. Others like to further separate their gear and prefer a divided bag. A few packs are available with a zip-out divider providing either option. The undivided bags often have compression straps to help stabilize smaller loads and prevent the gear from simply lumping up at the bottom of the bag. Entry into the bags also differs. Some are top loading and some front loading. Again, it seems to be a matter of personal preference. The bag size itself should suit your intentions. If most of the anticipated use will be the weekend to week-long travels, you won't require the largest expedition size models. There is the very old, but very reliable rule that a large volume pack will be filled to capacity. Whatever is carried that isn't essential soon becomes disgustingly heavy, especially when you know that you are the one responsible

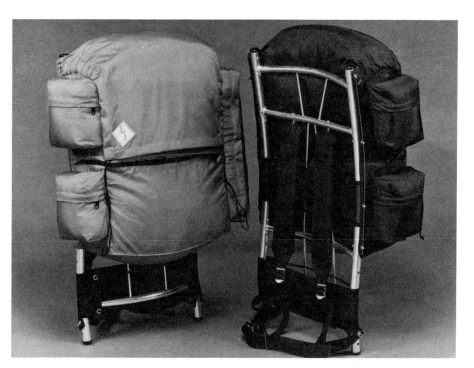

*The EMS* Divided Packer *and frame. Aluminum tubing frame is contoured to follow the shape of the spine. Divided packs are popular with hikers who like to separate their gear. Access to the bottom compartment is through a nylon coil zipper that extends across the back and between two of the side pockets.*

for loading it. Packs are available in a variety of sizes. There is no need to buy more, or less, than is appropriate to your use. Most packbags are made of weatherproofed material, although seam sealing is definitely recommended. For the truly drenching rains, two approaches seem most common. Some place all their gear in plastic bags and let it go at that. Otherwise, a waterproof rain cover is recommended. These urethane-coated nylon covers snap into place quickly and weigh about five to six ounces. Packbag zippers may be metal or nylon. The bag itself should be durable, well made, and well stitched with reinforcement at stress points. A number of items are standard on most packs or can be added. There are, for example, both stitched-on outside pockets and detachable pockets. There will be various lash points and loops for securing gear outside the pack.

The preferred, trail-loading system with frame packs places heavy items high in the pack and close to your back. Tents, stoves, fuel and food are typical items that may go high in the bag. A sleeping bag is rather light for its bulk and size and is usually at the bottom, secured outside the pack. The result of high and heavy packing keeps most of the weight pushing down on the hips as opposed to pulling down and out on the shoulders. Any small items that may be needed occasionally during the day may go just inside the pack or in one of the outside pockets.

Off-trail bushwhacking is a slightly different story, for potentially erratic footing calls for a lower center of gravity. Some packs can be lowered on their frames. Besides, items can be moved around in the pack to place the heavier items lower. Your shoulders should assume more of the weight in off-trail

*To some extent the soft, or internal frame pack overlaps and competes with the external frame pack. The soft pack is more suitable for off-trail situations where its closer riding, flexible characteristics provide enhanced balance. It is often chosen by winter hikers, cross country skiers, snowshoers and rock scramblers. The JanSport Mountain Spirit typifies the up-to-date design features of a well-planned internal frame pack.*

*Soft packs may need several fitting adjustments. A qualified local dealer can be of great help in selection and final fitting to the individual.*

situations. All of these changes will contribute to better balance for the questionable footing terrain you'll find in typical bushwhacking situations.

Although the external frame pack is the most widely used style, the past few years have witnessed a growing availability of soft, or internal, frame packs. To some extent use distinctions are becoming blurred and overlapped. Nevertheless, prevailing opinions suggest the external frame pack is the best trail travel choice. For those involved with cross country skiing, rock scrambling or a good deal of off-trail bushwhacking, the soft pack is preferable. It is more flexible and rides closer to the body. Several dealers reinforced these general impressions. Each advised that selection is being related primarily to the greatest intended use. The spring-through-fall trail travelers use external frame packs; the snow shoer, the cross country skier, the rock climber, and the determined bushwhacker choose the soft pack.

Soft packs are available in several designs. Usually there are internal supports: commonly flexible bars in a vertical or crisscrossed arrangement. The crisscrossed or "x" stays tend to give better support by pushing out the corners and permitting good response to body movement. There may be several adjustments in fitting the soft pack, and the experienced dealer is an invaluable aid in selection, fitting, and final adjustment.

If you are indecisive as to which style is most suitable for your purposes, it's best to define carefully your intended use. Then discuss the situation with a qualified dealer. Study the manufacturer's literature carefully. Most catalogs are very informative in outlining the intended uses of each pack design. As a final, conclusive comparison, arrange to rent each style on successive trips.

# 5.

# BOOTS

Proper boots are vital to the pleasure of any trip. Perhaps in recognition of their importance, continual controversy about the fine points of boot construction fills page after page in various magazines and books. As a result there is a wealth of fairly technical information floating around. If various manufacturers, with livelihoods dependent on providing the marketplace with durable, competetive values, can't agree on some fine points, I see no way to step in and knowledgeably arbitrate their differences. And, if the truth be known, I don't really want to know all there is to know about how to make a boot.

I do insist on a well-made, properly-fitted boot that will let me scramble over a variety of terrains and trail conditions, most often in the East, but often in the Midwest and West as well as the occasional trip out of the country. If this sounds casually careless, so be it. In practice it doesn't work out quite that way. I know the well-regarded brands; I know my feet, and I make sure of a proper fit. But sitting around a woodsy clearing and debating the merits of rough outs or smooth outs is about as much fun as listening to an insurance sales pitch.

Since there are more similarities than fine point differences, let's look briefly at the basic boot. Soles are a high-carbon, synthetic, rubber molded in a pattern of projecting lugs. *Vibram* is the usual brand. Over this lug sole you'll find a midsole of one or more layers, and finally the insole where your foot rests. Variable stitching methods are used to connect the sole to the upper boot. These upper boots are of specially selected and treated leather. Some are rough out; some smooth out. Arguments spin off relative to the merits of each, but in practice both work. Given some trial time, the appearances become similar. In any case, better boots use top grain, rather than split grain leather. There are single- or double-tongue closure systems. Bindings vary from eyelets, "D" rings, speed laces and hooks, usually singly but sometimes in combination. Some boots are cut higher than others and generally there is toe and heel hardness.

This seeming casualness assumes only one thing: that you are selecting a boot appropriate for general purpose backpacking. Although any backpacking shop is going to take proper care of you, it's good to be aware of what you won't be needing. You won't be buying specialized climbing boots, nor will you be looking at mountaineering boots where weight and rigidity contribute to warmth, support, security, and the execution of difficult maneuvers in specialized terrain. It's the general purpose backpacking boot that will treat you well when you've got that twenty to forty pounds or more on your back. We'll touch on some of the lighter weight alternatives presently, but for now we'll concentrate on a well-constructed boot that will stand up well enough so that at least one set of replacement soles will be needed before any other part of the boot wears out. Generally, you're looking for a boot to come in at no more than four and a half pounds, and possibly less in a medium size nine example.

The army has determined that a pound on your feet is as hard to move as five pounds on your back. Consequently experienced hikers try to find boots just heavy enough for their intended use, but no heavier.

The fortunate will hit on the right boot at the first shot. Others are in for a fairly long fitting session. Whatever time it takes is worth it, as proper fit is essential. Be sure to bring or wear the sock combination that you will use on the trail. Two pair are preferred. Some like a medium weight wool athletic sock with a heavier Ragg wool outer sock. Others prefer a light, nylon, inner sock under the heavier wick wool sock. In any case, the two pairs cushion the feet while walking, reduce the chance of blisters, help keep the feet dry, and provide resilience as your feet swell with the passing miles.

Sales people in backpacking shops tend to be hikers themselves and will discuss knowingly your boot requirements. They'll obtain accurate foot measurements as the session gets underway. Don't worry about a generalized fit, whether the boot is of American or European origin. Most European boots built for the North American market respect the anatomy of the typical American foot, which is apparently somewhat different than the average European shape. Incidentally, many boots are built on women's lasts or patterns and, in some cases, women will find satisfaction with a man's version. Something for everyone exists. If you know one foot is larger than the other, start the fittings with the larger foot. In most shops the finger fit method is used as a starting point. There should be at least half an inch, but less than an inch, ahead of your stockinged foot. With the boot unlaced, push the foot forward as far as possible. The index finger should just fit down between the heel and the heel cup or back of the boot. Next, with the heel all the way back in the boots, lace them tightly. Did the laces pull the closures so tightly that they almost touched? If so, the boot is too loose. Is the arch length comfortable? If everything checks out okay to this point, stand to do a couple of knee bends. This will indicate heel fit. You'll want a firm fit. A very slight heel lift of about an eighth of an inch is okay.

## BOOT CONSTRUCTION

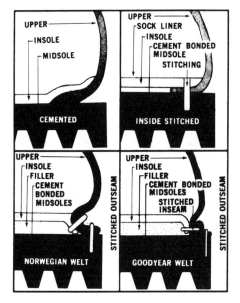

**Cemented** construction involves folding and gluing an upper between the narrow insole and sole Cemented boots are flexible, but lack good protection and usually cannot be resoled.

**Inside Stitched** or **Littleway** constructed boots have the upper sandwiched between the inner sole and midsole. These layers are fastened together by a double row of lock stitching, providing a closely cropped sole. These boots are relatively stiff.

**Norwegian** welt construction has several rows of stitching along the boot perimeter where sole meets upper. One row angles inward, connecting insole with upper; the other secures upper to the midsoles. This is the strongest type of boot construction.

In **Goodyear** welt construction, the upper is stitched to the insole and to the welt, which runs along the boot perimeter where sole meets upper. Welt is then stitched to midsole.

Confirming checks on heel lift can be done on an available stair tread. Otherwise, the sales person can hold the heel to the floor while you attempt to lift the back of the foot. A different check is for someone to hold the foot down. Try to rotate the foot inside the boot. The ball of the foot should not shift noticeably sideways. Don't worry if it feels slightly snug in this dimension. Boots will work in a bit here, but a boot that's loose before use will lead to troubling abrasiveness later. If everything is still going well, try to simulate uphill and downhill walking. Many stores have a slant ramp. If not, kick hard against a solid object or hook the heel over a stair tread and point the foot steeply downward. You want to confirm that the toes won't stub against the toe of the boot.

Wear the boots for several minutes around the store. Repeat the bends, twists, and slant-ramp checks. How is the feel above the ankle? It should be snug but not biting. Heavier boots may have a scree cuff or padded collar. Lighter boots may not, but the lightweight boot leather can be expected to break in well and contour to the ankle. Even if everything seems correct, it's wise to discuss the possibility of a return. Can you take them home to try out inside. If they show wear you'll end up with a pair of novel bookends or planters depending on your wife's current interior decorating scheme. Also I'll leave it to you to explain any new and mysterious black marks that appear on the kitchen floor.

Okay, to review the high points: correct length, half an inch or barely more ahead of your stocked foot; comfortable height over the instep; correct arch length; snug, not sloppy width; no appreciable heel lift. Everything is okay on the up and downhill simulations, no painful bite above the ankle, and an okay from the store to exchange if blisters erupt from in-home wear. And last, trust the foot feedback you're getting. Don't be enamored with a particular brand so that you're tempted to force fit them to your feet. Any boot that doesn't fit correctly won't break in satisfactorily. It will find a way to bite back and break you instead.

If there is no local supplier nearby, you can purchase your boots satisfactorily by mail from the larger catalog houses. They provide complete ordering information and illustrate how a pattern tracing of your foot may be taken. You know your feet. If you have a high instep, unusual width, length, or other potential problem, you had best make a special trip to a reliable shop for the personalized help of an experienced fitter. Otherwise, there should be no problem in ordering by mail. If nothing else works, there are custom bootmakers you can turn to. Their work will be costly but superbly done.

Normally the downtown shoe store has no real place in selection. They are fine for the lightweight alternatives: sneakers, work boots or whatever. However, even if they handle a brand or two of quality boots, they tend to lack the specialized fitting knowledge. The single exception that comes to mind is a replacement boot for the experienced hiker who can fit himself.

When the boot is selected and deemed appropriate, find out from the sales clerk or the maker's literature whether the boots were oil tanned (also known as vegetable tanned) or chrome tanned. It makes a difference in the water protective process you should initially use. If oil tanned, use boot grease or boot oil applied by generous rubbing (in other words, rub long and hard). If chrome tanned, use one of the silicone waxes such as *SnoSeal*, again rubbing generously.

*Two popular boot models from Vasque. Manufacturer recommendations suggest: model 6230 (left),* Hiker II, *for rugged back country hiking and backpacking; model 7506 (right),* Cascade, *for lighter weight hiking.*

The breaking-in process will take time and slowly accumulated mileage. Start gradually, work up, and don't take seriously to the trail until the boots are well broken in. If time is a factor, fill the boots with hot water and empty right away. Wearing the dry socks you'll be using on a regular trail trip, go out and walk them dry. The effect is a concentrated dose of what your own feet would accomplish over a longer time period. The moisture will work naturally through the leather. When they are dry they should be just about set. It sounds squishy, but I've worn so many waders that have leaked over a period of years that my feet are almost webbed. This process is much warmer than leaky boots in an April trout stream.

Maintain the boots well. If they get unavoidably wet on the trail, change to dry socks and walk the boots dry. If it's late in the day, just turn the boots upside down and let them dry at their natural speed. Don't use extra heat which is destructive to all parts of the boot. Any caked mud can be removed with a stiff wire brush.

Clean the boots between trips. If they are wet and muddy, sponge them off and brush them. Allow them to dry naturally. Some hikers hasten the process by stuffing them with paper. When dry, saddlesoap the interior and use *Sno-Seal* or an equivelent on the outside. This time it's okay for both oil and chrome tanned boots. Be sparing, though, and don't overdo it. Some hikers place shoe trees in the boots. Someplace them on ski racks. For prolonged storage, many place the boots in plastic bags and seal them.

How about lightweight alternatives? The so-called work boots that often feature a padded interior, smooth outers, and heavy crepe soles are pretty good. Indeed, many hikers never go heavier. Jogging shoes and sneakers are seen with some regularity. Generally, if the trips are short and pack weights not excessive, these alternatives work out pretty well. All of them lack the true support of a good boot, but if they work for you, fine. In good conscience, no experienced packer is going to recommend them, but there is also no denying that some people are quite satisfied with these choices. Another popular alternative for wet areas or trips when you can expect combined wet and cold is the L.L. Bean hunting boot.

Other on-trail footwear considerations might involve booties, moccasins, or low-cut sneakers for those around-the-camp moments. Many hikers bring foot powder as the feet deserve every consideration. They got you there and they have to get you back in comfort.

Overall, the best down-to-basics boot selection advice I've heard occured a few years ago when I was "gainfully employed" as Technical Director at Orvis. At the time we handled backpacking items as well as a primary line of fishing tackle. Having something to discuss with one of our showroom people, I went into the store. The salesman I wanted to see was involved with fitting a pair of boots to a boy in his mid-teens. I stood by to wait until the salesman was free. The concerned mother of the boy also hovered nearby. The boy was apparently unconvinced that the outdoor life was going to be for him as he constantly scowled and frowned during the fitting. Finally he stood and clomped around the showroom for a few minutes. As he came back and sat down, his mother inquired how the boots felt. The boy shrugged his shoulders, frowned indifferently, and threw up his hands slightly. Mother, in her infinite wisdom, said, "Not to worry, Marvin. They're for walking, not for fancy."

This is really what boot selection is all about.

# 6.

# TENTS

There are inexpensive, short-term answers to wilderness shelter as well as the more standard, walled-tent alternatives. Most people start with the security of a tent, but there will come a night, mild and star filled, when the tent will be joyfully ignored in favor of the open world. Still, lying there like a pupating butterfly is not an adequate overall answer for weather and insect protection.

Cost is ultimately going to play a very real part in the final shelter decision, so let's work our way up this shaky ladder of shelter alternatives and look first at some low cost possibilities. About the simplest is an inexpensive tarp. Essentially it is a single, waterproof, grommeted fly, that can be erected in a variety of configurations. As a temporary solution, even a large three mil (.003) or four mil (.004) polyethylene sheet can be used. When carefully rigged, tarps provide surprisingly good rain protection—although it's tough to handle insect populations. Next step is the inexpensive, open-ended, tube tent. A one person model is typically about nine feet long and perhaps a bit over three feet in diameter. These provide better side protection than offered by a simple tarp and some tube tents are available with insect screening at each end.

None of these are a completely adequate, long-term solution for privacy and weather protection for which a tent must ultimately be considered. Borrowing or renting may be sensible before making the final investment decision of a tent of your own. First time equipment purchasers often find it easy to overestimate what they really need in terms of weight, durability, and protection. Even though a lot of equipment is oversold, realistically (at least half the time) the problem lies with the consumer and an understandable tendency to overestimate, through inexperience, the conditions with which he will be involved. As a result, he feels better protected through overbuying. I'm not implying that caution isn't good, but simply that your bombproof winter model that will stand up to a gale is hot and heavy on a July weekend in the Catskills. Current costs are high enough to demand a wise, initial selection. A well-made tent with reasonable care will provide years of faithful service. Just be as realistic as possible about the demands you will make of the equipment. Some considerations are: How much use is the tent going to receive? Where will it be used most often? Under what average weather conditions? How many people will it be required to sleep? How easy is it to pitch? How stable is it in the expected weather range? What, if any at all, unusual features are required? What is the apparent quality, overall workmanship, and price?

Starting with the elusive standpoint of cost, many moderately priced tents are single-walled, waterproof models. Here is where the potential for argument begins. I say potential only because experienced packers usually don't argue much about them. They automatically dismiss these choices.

A pint of water vapor is produced while sleeping through the combination of perspiring and exhaling. With two people confined in a small area on a hot, humid night, a quart or more of water vapor will be produced. That water vapor condenses on the waterproof interior and may drip back down on you.

*Interior condensation problems must be expected with coated, waterproof tents, no matter how roomy, lightweight and moderately priced.*

Well, I'll buy that as fact, but I don't buy the arbitrary, automatic dismissal of this tent type. For many people and many conditions these can be good values. The price is moderate, they are usually lightweight and roomy, and if they are well ventilated the condensation problems can be minimized, though not eliminated. Still there are occasional sticky nights, especially in the East and Midwest, when it's hot enough to cook a duck. Anything short of air conditioning would be inadequate. That might be the night to break free of the walled restraint and sample the uniqueness of a star-filled night. There's no law that says you have to sleep in the tent. In brief, even if everything else you read and hear says to ignore these tents, make that decision slowly for serious backpacking, especially if price is going to be a factor in your ultimate decision.

The next step up is the standard wilderness tent. The usual offering is a main shelter of mostly permeable nylon so moisture can escape; above this, a separate waterproof fly is attached. Usually, but not always, the two parts are separated and you can leave one or the other unused in some conditions. The primary tent alone does a good job when the weather is agreeable. A rainfly used alone makes a fine tarp. In cool weather the tent and fly in normal combination add to the obtainable warmth inside the tent. In wet conditions the tent and fly combination affords the best weather protection.

Tents are available in several sizes. The usual concern is with two-man or three-man models. In a pinch most two-man models will passably, but not ideally, handle three. Some hikers prefer three-man models even when traveling as a pair, feeling the extra roominess is compensation enough for the added weight factors. In general, a three season tent can weigh about three pounds or a bit more per person. Thus a two-man model can reasonably come in close to six pounds; a three-man model around nine pounds.

In a categorical oversimplification, there are three-season tents and specialized winter tents. The latter are superb examples of the tent makers abilities, but they are more tent than we normally require. The three-season models come in various configurations, but the "A" frame style with rectangular floor area is still the most common. This low-profile "A" frame utilizes a level roof line or one that slopes from head to toe. Structurally, the concept uses poles thrust through fabric sleeves along each side of the "A" frame front. At the foot may be another "A" frame, although a short "I" post is also common. Simpler versions may use an "I" post at each end, but the "A" frame front provides a more stable arrangement.

The usual tent construction is nylon taffeta or ripstop nylon. The floor extends several inches up the sides and is waterproof. Above the waterproof tub floor the breathable nylon takes over. The waterproof fly is attached above the tent. Ventilation and insect screening are important, and the various manufacturers' solutions generally are quite satisfactory. The floor of the tent receives the greatest use. Consequently, it's a good idea to pitch the tent over a groundcloth.

Returning for a moment to the concept of the waterproof tent, we are witnessing the introduction of several tents incorporating *Gore-Tex* to provide that theoretical ideal of a breathable, yet waterproof, single-wall model. Increased costs must be expected, but this certainly deserves consideration in your final selection.

*The* Taku Tent *utilizes an innovative design combined with* Gore-Tex *material to provide waterproof protection without requiring a separate fly. The Taku is a two-person design with a total weight of 4 lbs., 14 oz.*

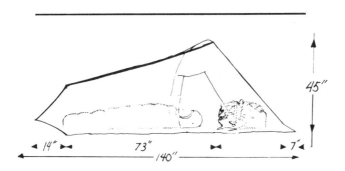

## TAKU TENT

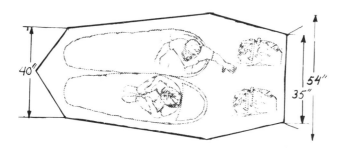

*The* Trail Dome *(shown with fly in place) is a roomy design for two persons with all their gear or three persons with minimum gear inside. Dome shapes allow good headroom and flexible interior arrangements of sleeping bags, hiking gear, and small equipment items.*

There are other design ideas besides the standard "A" frame concept. Most of them attempt to provide increased head room through various dome shapes. Increasingly popular and increasingly available, these new design ideas deserve attention before the final choice is made.

Tent color? In a word—variable. Personal choice plays the dominant role. Can you be happy for a few days or a few weeks (or not at all) in blaze orange? Would you prefer to blend into the landscape with a more subdued coloration? Whichever direction you wish to take, conspicuous or subdued seems to be available today.

A tent is a long-term and important consideration. Going slowly and going thoroughly is going wisely.

# 7.

# SLEEPING BAGS

Many will argue that the sleeping bag is the single most important item among the basics of boots, pack, tent, and sleeping bag. Whether it is or not may be debatable, but the fact that it is arguable at all indicates the reliance experienced hikers place on a suitable sleeping bag.

There are three general classifications of sleeping bags: the mild weather or recreational bag of limited use, the three-season category, and the winter-capable models. Broadly speaking, we are concerned with the three-season selections, for these coincide with our normal angling potentials. Even this premise, helpful as a starting point, leaves several determinations to be made such as comfort rating, filler material, loft, weight, construction features, shape, and cost. Although each aspect may have some bearing on the final selection, there should be no single overriding feature that dictates the final choice. The final selection should incorporate the best combination of features appropriate to the intended use of the bag.

When comparing sleeping bags, you should first note an assigned comfort rating. I doubt that any company is totally comfortable with assigning such a rating. They always point out that this is simply an attempt to realistically average out a normal, healthy person's ability to sleep warmly and comfortably. The problem with such a rating is the number of variables, both of metabolic and environmental considerations. Some people simply sleep warmer than others; whether you have eaten just before retiring also makes a difference (i.e., you'll sleep warmer with a late snack). Relative humidity, the wind and the amount of shelter from the wind, as well as ground insulation and the amount of clothing worn to bed are elastic variables. The makers must also consider the amount of loft and the shape of the bag before assigning any comfort rating determination. As a result, any assigned comfort rating should only be taken as one potentially influencing factor in bag selection.

Sleeping bags have changed quite a bit in the past few years. At one point prime goose down filled virtually all fine bags. In recent years several factors have diluted this influence and such singular dominance no longer exists. The availability of prime goose down has been greatly reduced. The best quality down comes from older birds, and recent marketing trends have caused the birds to be harvested much earlier in their life. Along with the reduced availability has been a parallel and dramatic increase in cost. Prime goose down was, and indeed remains, highly regarded for its light weight, loft, compressive ability, resiliency, warmth, and long life.

Another development since the early seventies has been the introduction and gradual acceptance of duck down as an alternative. Duck down has similar properties but does not loft quite as well. Currently there are bags incorporating goose down only, combinations of goose and duck down, duck down only, and even some bags using down and synthetic alternatives. These provide down above the sleeper and polyester alternatives beneath the sleeper.

Then there are the polyester alternatives themselves. The two materials with current broad acceptance are *Hollofill II®* and *Polarguard®*. *Polarguard* is a continuous filament structure while *Hollofill II* represents masses of short fibers. Although advantages are proclaimed for each, they are similar in loft and compression qualities. Both, like down, must be stabilized within the shell of the bag to prevent shifting and resulting cold spot development. Both materials are widely available and may be said to share some advantages and some disadvantages when compared to down. Functionally, their most important advantage is warmth when wet. Down loses its loft when wet. A well-soaked down bag is useless! The synthetics absorb very small amounts of moisture. Even a thoroughly soaked bag can be wrung out and still provide efficient protection. The drying time of a soaked polyester bag is also much more rapid than the drying time of a wet down bag. The potential for a soggy sleeping bag is probably greater than the new hiker might imagine. Some regions and/or seasons are quite wet or have humid, damp climates. A stream crossing stumble or a leaky tent during a prolonged rain are further occurrances in backcountry travel.

*Synthetic fill bags are less expensive than down and offer excellent warmth-when-wet capabilities which may be important for hikers in humid, damp regions. This model is from Eastern Mountain Sports.*

If price considerations are important, the advantage lies with the synthetics. They are considerably less expensive.

Regardless of filler material, the sleeping bag must be constructed to keep that filler from shifting and developing unwelcome cold spots. Down filler is loose, so various inner walls or baffles are used to keep the down from shifting. In most quality bags there are three basic approaches and a few individual company variations of these basics. The three concepts are box, slant wall and "V" tube construction. The box is least common and not as well regarded as the others. It consists of a series of internal walls at right angles to the bag shell. There is a greater chance of fill shifting and resultant cold spot development with the box construction when compared to the alternatives of slant wall and "V" tube construction. The slant wall is common in quality down bags because it does a better job of limiting down migration while permitting full loft. This method employs interior baffles set at a slant or angle to the bag shell. The "V" tube construction is a series of triangular or V-shaped walls in an alternating series of both upside down V's and right side up V's. This is also a well regarded and very effective method of limiting down fill migration. This construction is more costly to manufacture than slant wall construction as there is both more material and labor involved.

In the polyester bags there are also variable solutions to the potential of filler material shifting. Double quilting is one. Two layers are atop each other. The seams may lie above each other but a preferred method offsets them, permitting one thin wall to backed by a thick wall. Edge stabilization is another solution. The batt is sewn to the inner shell around its edges to eliminate sewn-through seams which could cause cold spots to develop. Usually the sewing is along the drawstring tube at the neck and hood and at the zipper seam. There is a possibility of a shifting shell fabric with edge stabilization. The best regarded solution is sandwich construction. This combines good features from both edge stabilization and double quilting. One batt is quilted to each of the two shell fabrics, then one or two additional batts are placed between the quilted layers and sewn around their edges to the inner shell. The potential discomfort of a shifting shell fabric is eliminated, and you have a warmer bag since less of the polyester filler is compressed by stabilizing seams. Again, individual companies may offer their modified interpretations of these basic concepts, but overall these are the primary methods employed by the industry.

Regardless of filler material, the workmanship of any quality bag is important. Any potential stress areas should be examined carefully. Check for good, even tension where the bag is sewn. Most specialists recommend about eight to ten stitches per inch. They feel fewer stitches may not be adequate while too many stitches may weaken the material itself. If you are particularly fastidious, you might check inside the bag at the foot area. This is the most difficult area to sew.

Zippers should run from top to bottom with the ability to open from either end. Nylon zippers are lighter than metal and do not conduct the cold as metal might. Similar bags or zipper-compatible models can be zippered together. Just be sure to purchase one bag with a right zipper and one bag with a left zipper. A good draft tube should run the length of the zipper. This filled tube will prevent cold from entering.

Material loft is still another consideration. Lofting can be measured in cubic inches filled by an ounce of material. Depending on type and quality, down may loft from about 400 to perhaps 625 or 650 inches. To establish some slightly arbitrary benchmarks, let's say good quality down will loft in the area of 500 to 550 inches and today's premium down about 625 to 650. Comparatively, the polyester alternatives may come in about 350 cubic inches. From the standpoint of efficiency, the more inches of loft per pound of total weight, the better off you are. Down is clearly the leader here, for synthetic bags require more filler to provide equal protection. This translates to a real but not extraordinary difference in weight. If we were to compare two bags of similar shape from the same manufacturer, one of down and one of a polyester alternative, we'd probably find about a thirty percent weight difference, give or take a couple of percent. The actual weight difference might be from a pound to almost two pounds in favor of down. On the trail, however, the actual weight of complete sleeping systems might be a bit less than this. Down compresses more beneath the sleeper, so a thicker or heavier sleeping bag may be desired with the down bag.

In connection with loft there is one more consideration which hasn't yet evolved into a trend, but which is common enough to warrant looking into. This is loft placement. Commonly we're used to half the material above the sleeper, half below. Some current offerings redistribute this and provide more filler above the sleeper and less below. Such loft placement could have bearing on bag selection.

Regardless of filler material, sleeping bags are available in similar shape offerings. The slimmest profile is the standard mummy bag; then we shade off into slightly roomier versions. They may be called by different names, but essentially they are barrel, semirectangular, and rectangular. Shape has a bearing on both weight and function. A bag is a heat loss barrier around the body. The roomier the bag is, the less efficient it is. The most confining profile will provide the most warmth for the least amount of fill. For this reason the mummy bag is the usual recommendation. With less air space for the body to warm, it has the most efficient shape. Some find the mummy bag too confining for comfort and look to the just slightly roomier versions of barrel or semirectangular offerings. The general recommendation then comes down to this: Select the narrowest bag that you find for adequate comfort.

Normally sleeping bags have been made of permeable fabrics, allowing moisture to pass away from the body. A new approach challenges this concept via the introduction of a vapor barrier liner. Advocates of this concept maintain there will be more warmth obtained without getting wet. To be comfortable the body should maintain a layer of humid air next to the skin. Normally this tends to dry out and sweating occurs, partially to recharge it with moisture. At the same time some evaporative heat loss occurs.

By sleeping with a vapor barrier, the air by the skin quickly becomes humid

Gore-Tex *shells are a new development and are being used on some down bags to provide dryness in damp seasons and regions.*

*Another relatively new concept is the Bivouac sack. These "bivvy sacks" can provide a minimum weight solo shelter or can be used over your bag in tent for added warmth and dryness. This offering,* The Burrow, *has* Gore-Tex *material for weather protection.*

and stays that way as sweating slows down and evaporative body heat loss is reduced. One advocate, *Camp 7*, offers the concept this way: a light down bag is used inside a larger bag of *Polarguard*; a separate, removable, nylon liner goes between you and the sleeping bag. They point out in their catalog that each bag, of down and of *Polarguard*, can be used separately as well as in the above described combination.

Owners of down bags concerned with moisture problems can look to some new materials and concepts. Some bags now have *Gore-Tex*® shells. Also, a *Gore-Tex* bivy sack can be used with a regular down bag. Add a vapor-barrier liner, and down bag users should remain dry without any problems.

Along with the sleeping bag of your choice are some related items. If you decide to go tentless on a mild weather trip you will want a ground cloth beneath the bag. A sleeping pad is also desirable to protect you from the hardness of the ground and to provide some insulating value. Closed cell pads are popular and available in a variety of lengths, widths, and thicknesses. Summer conditions are the easiest—most prefer a short pad of about four feet and a thickness of perhaps $\frac{1}{4}$ to $\frac{3}{8}$ of an inch. Cooler weather in the spring or fall might require a longer, heavier pad.

There are also open cell pads in waterproof covers. They too are available in variable lengths and thicknesses. They are considered quite comfortable, but they are bulkier.

Some hikers prefer an air mattress. The better types feature separate air tubes. If there is a single air valve and interconnected tubes, one puncture leaves you without any protection. In colder weather air mattresses are less satisfactory, for air circulates within them and carries some body heat away from you. There is even a self-inflating air mattress said to combine the best features of a foam pad and an air mattress. A waterproof nylon shell contains a special lightweight open cell foam. As the valve is opened, the foam expands and fills the mattress. Then it is topped off with a breath or two. The inflated dimensions of one such offering are $48 \times 19 \times 1\frac{1}{2}$ inches, it weighs one pound, eight ounces, and the price is currently $32.00. Comparatively, one closed-cell pad from the same catalog has dimensions of $42 \times 18\frac{1}{2} \times 14$ inches, with a weight of six ounces, and a $4.00 price. An open cell pad at $48 \times 20 \times 1\frac{1}{2}$ inches weighs one pound, eight ounces, and carries a $13.00 price. Another alternative is a combination pad of $\frac{1}{4}$ inch of closed cell and $1\frac{1}{4}$ inch of open cell. This offering at $48 \times 20 \times 1\frac{1}{2}$ inches, weighs one pound, ten ounces, and has a current price of $15.00.

For a pillow, some prefer an inflatable model. Most hikers probably still jam some clothing into a stuff bag and let it go at that.

The essentials of your sleeping bag selection are sufficient roominess for your personal comfort, warmth and comfort enough for the anticipated temperature ranges, and light weight enough to pack well and stuff compactly. Finally, if humidity or moisture is a regional/seasonal consideration, be protected accordingly.

# 8.

# THE OUTDOOR KITCHEN

## Camp Stoves

A traditional part of the wilderness experience has always been the small cook fire, and not without understandable reason. The flickering flames generate an almost subliminal atmosphere and comfort after a long day. Food preparation, warmth, and those elusive emotional aspects of fire are legitimate reasons for fire—at least they have been.

Now there are real and ethical reasons for minimizing the use of fire in many areas, and the total prohibition of fire in other areas. The vast increase in wilderness use of recent years has led to inevitable abuse. The numerous firespots in more popular landscapes are at first glance ridiculous, then appalling. Increasing areas are being closed to fire and further restrictions are inevitable. Still we should not be extremist in our case. There are some situations and locations where the careful handling of a fire cannot be detrimental to the land. Your strictest conscience coupled with appropriate conditions are the criteria for this determination. Fire may be reasonable in moist wooded areas that are heavily littered with down and dead wood. For the angler, some of the gravelly river banks are other possible sites, especially when they are located below high water marks, or in sites where fire marks may be easily erased.

Still, twinges of aesthetic regret aside, the stove is a requirement of every wilderness party, as modern realisms and demands can only be met by their use. There is no concern about gathering wood. This saves time and broadens the scope of potential camp sites. Meal preparation is quicker, more convenient, and efficient. Stoves also have an inherent simplicity of operation.

Backpackers often say that a particular style of stove is harder to start than another, but it is all relative. True, each stove seems to have its own quirks, yet none of them is all that difficult to start for ordinary backpacking use. Some chill morning you'll treasure that convenience as you pry yourself halfway out of the sleeping bag, reach over and start the stove roaring to prepare coffee.

Since a stove is essential, it is worth taking your time in deciding which model is for you. Among your many considerations are: fuel type and availability; weight of the stove and fuel; overall compatability with your intended use; stability, packing ease, safety and operational ease; poor weather performance; boiling time and average operational time before refilling; simmering ability; quality of the product (how well it is made and its apparent overall durability). Since none of the stoves for average backpacking are excessively expensive, cost may be the last consideration.

*Modern demands require each wilderness party to carry a stove. The* Peak 1 *from Coleman is a white gas model offering high performance and reliability for the three season requirements of the angler/packer.*

The first choice to make is fuel type. Although backpacking stoves are available in several models, there are three primary designs based on the fuel type consumed: the white gas models; the butane or propane types that use prefilled, pressurized fuel cannisters; and there are some kerosene models.

White gas stoves are probably regarded as the old standard since reliable models have been around for quite some time. The white gas normally referred to by backpackers is "camp fuel," available in various brands, most commonly known as *Coleman Fuel*. This is a cleaner fuel than raw white gas because it contains additives and rust inhibitors for easier lighting and cleaner burning qualities. It is generally available nationwide, stocked by most backpacking shops as well as many hardware stores and general sporting goods outlets. On the plus side for white gas models: They are generally lightweight, fuel is easily available, and any spilled gas will evaporate quickly. On the minus side for these stoves: Priming is required (above freezing priming is not required by some) and any spilled fuel, while it does evaporate quickly, is highly flammable.

Kerosene models are not as popular for general backpacking as white gas or cannister types. Nonetheless, some kerosene models are available in this country. For travel outside North American areas, it may be the only fuel readily available. The fuel is less volatile than white gas, but once it gets going it burns even hotter. Spilled fuel doesn't tend to flare into a flash fire, but kerosene models require careful priming and the fuel isn't as clean as white gas. Spilled fuel evaporates slowly, and stoves are somewhat harder to get started.

Butane and propane both come in prefilled, pressurized cartridges. Of the two, butane is the most widely used. Propane requires very heavy cartridges. While it flows in colder weather, propane is infrequently used for ordinary backpacking. Both are similar in that they are liquids under pressure. On leaving the cannister they are vaporized and ready to burn. Butane models are easier to light in a wind, require no priming period, fuel won't spill, and immediate heat is available. However, the fuel is relatively expensive, cartridges are comparatively heavy, and empty ones must be packed out of the woods. There is a lower heat output which lengthens cooking times, and as the cannisters empty they cool to further reduce the stove's efficiency.

Fuel compatability with your intended use is also important. A short summer trip, say going solo for a day or two, probably means you won't be doing much more than boiling up a few cups of water. You may elect for the convenient aspects of butane in such a case. A large group, especially a mixed group of adults and children may be influenced by the somewhat safer aspects of kerosene. There may be several careless people around the cooking area. The basic stove for the angler/packer may be one of the white gas models.

Just as most anglers end up with more than one fly rod, owning two stoves ultimately makes sense. One friend handles it this way. He occasionally takes off solo for a day or two in the mountains and keeps everything to a minimum. For this he uses a lightweight propane model. For longer trips, or when traveling with a companion, he carries his white gas stove.

Once the fuel type and its compatability with your intentions is determined, you can look to the other features mentioned which will ultimately lead to the most satisfactory stove for you. Quality backpacking shops and various catalogs can help in sizing up different competetive features. Specialty magazines, such as the excellent *Backpacker*, run periodic equipment appraisals that are quite comprehensive in their scope.

All portable stoves come with directions for starting, maintenance, and repair considerations. In actual practice, each stove seems to have its own characteristics. Become familiar with the operation of a newly acquired stove before setting out for the backcountry. Set it up in the yard a few times, run it at various burning levels, and determine average fuel supply times. In short, become familiar and comfortable with the stove. You will rely heavily on it. Despite an inherent simplicity of operation, any stove must be completely understood, handled carefully, and respected as potentially dangerous.

# Cooking Utensils

This is an area in which it's understandably easy to overequip. The stores and catalogs offer a variety of items that seem practical and convenient, until you've added them to the pack and lugged them around long enough to decide you can do without them. Regardless of how you start, the items you ultimately end up with as your basic utensils probably will be somewhat different, or at least modified and simplified. All you really need is a functional, lightweight minimum of gear that will meet your needs and cooking and eating preferences. Overequipping wastes space, adds extra weight and adds to meal clean up chores when there are better things to do.

Although there may be some useful lightweight items around the house, the usual starting point is a stove and matching cook set. A couple of well-known examples are the Coleman *Peak 1* stove and optional matching cook set and the Sigg *Tourist Cook Kit* which provides a pair of pots, a combination lid-fry pan, potgripper and supportive base-windscreen for the *Svea 123*. There are several other brands, and items may be purchased as a complete set or individually.

Cook sets should be convenient and nest together for easy packing. They may be used as is or as part of an overall cook set. Be sure to have a potgripper (little pliers with a right angle head), or a bandana handy—you'll remember the first time you burn your fingers. A nonstick fry pan with a folding handle or detachable handle is handy, and some pot lids do double duty as fry pans. A ladle or serving spoon, plastic or metal cups and spoons suffice for most trail menus.

There can be more. Some like plastic or aluminum plates or bowls, or both. If you want one, take the bowls. They are the most practical choice. Plastic may keep food warmer longer than aluminum. There are also knife, fork, and spoon sets that hook together. A part of this you'll lose—I don't know how, or why, but you will. When you do, lose the fork first, then if you must, the knife. Most hikers carry a couple of knives anyway (say a Swiss Army model and a larger folding knife). Inexpensive, two-part salt and pepper shakers are handy. Many hikers have learned to take advantage of the fast food chains by picking up individual helpings of jam, jelly, mustard, ketchup, etc. The hard to handle items such as peanut butter, jam, mayonnaise, etc. can go into plastic squeeze tubes. Spoon them in, fold, and slide on the locking clip. The herbs, spices, etc. are carried in 35mm film cans, poly vials, old pill bottles, or ziploc bags.

Food usually goes into plastic bags. There are also various sized plastic boxes. Canned goods aren't a usual part of backpacking, but a number of hikers seem to like a can of sardines. A cheap G.I. can opener is useful if there isn't an opener on your knife.

Large, collapsible, water carriers may be helpful. There are several alternatives for liquids: aluminum and plastic bottles, baby bottles and various canteens.

*The well-made and convenient* Sigg Tourist Cook Kit *is shown with the* Sigg *Fuel Bottle and* Svea 123 stove. *(Eastern Mountain Sports)*

Beyond the basics there are new backpacker ovens which I haven't tried yet but should prove to be excellent with the new add-water-only biscuit and coffee cake mixes. Some special situations, such as high altitude cooking or very long treks, may involve you with a pressure cooker. A four quart version weighs about three pounds. It is not an ordinary backpacking item, yet most stoves aren't as efficient at high altitudes and the boiling point of water is altered. Fuel savings under these circumstances may be substantial enough to more than make up for the weight of the pressure cooker. As a common item, members of your party should take turns carrying it.

Some hikers like to bring a small tea kettle. Among other oddities, even the ancient Chinese Wok is showing up along the trails. Without doubt, if an item can be carried, it has been in the woods somewhere, somehow.

Finally, a few random odds and ends in connection with utensils. Aluminum foil can be a helpful addition to the kit. Somewhat blackened pots and pans will hold and distribute heat better, so don't worry about their exterior appearance. Buy or make stuff bags for them if they were not a prt of your original purchase. You don't want soot or carbon deposits all over the rest of your gear. If you still feel uneasy, place the stuff sacks in heavy duty plastic bags. Have lots of extra plastic bags of various sizes. They end up being used in a number of ways. Clean the interior of pots and pans carefully. You don't want bacteria affecting your system forty miles from nowhere. Nylon scrub pads are handy, and many hikers bring along a biodegradable soap for cleanup. Never dump used wash water into any water source.

If you will be having a fire at some point, a backpacker's grill is a handy item; you can substitute a light cake rack from home if the use is just occasional, as it probably should be. Don't overlook *Sterno* as a backup stove and as a handy item when you're a couple of miles upstream from the established camp and you'd like some soup for lunch. It's slow but it does the job eventually.

Finally, in some parts of the wilderness, bears can be a problem. Have enough cord and a stout container to use for bear bagging. This will be done at some distance from your established camp. About the easiest method is to tie a rock to one end of the cord and heave it over a horizontal branch some distance above the ground. Next, place the food in whatever container you have chosen, and tie it to the end of the cord where the stone was. Haul the sack up into position, and anchor the hauling end around a tree trunk. In some of the real problem areas, bears have gotton very smart about this, so many people recommend dual anchors. If you are successful in finding a good, high, horizontal branch, try to end up with the supporting container about fifteen feet above the ground, a few feet below the supporting branch and several feet away from the nearest, anchoring tree trunk.

# Fire

The day of the indiscriminate fire is over. Every wilderness party should have a stove. This is indisputable, yet there are times when fire may be appropriate or even a necessity. If you're out of fuel, fire may be required for food preparation. In cold, wet weather, it may be useful for drying clothes and regaining some semblance of comfort. Therefore, even if you subscribe wholeheartedly to the new fire use realism, you should know something about locating and starting a camp fire.

As a routine procedure, always check the fire regulations and conditions of the area in which you will be traveling in advance. The criteria that make a fire acceptable under normal circumstances are an existing, well-located fire site and an abundance of down and dead wood. Be cautious of possible wind-blown sparks, and don't locate too close to your tent, other equipment, or dry underbrush. Don't locate on a promontory or exposed shelf. The wind that springs up when the fire is going fans the flames and makes them burn well—too well. These fires heat poorly as cool air is constantly replacing the warm air. More importantly, the possibility of dangerous wind-blown sparks increases. Don't locate a new fire next to a tree or atop vegetation in heavily forested areas. It could mean igniting subterranean root structures which might smolder unseen for days before resurfacing some distance away from the original site.

A new fire is best sited on bare ground, gravelly areas, or sand where fire marks may be easily erased. Beaches and gravelly shores are also adequate, especially when the fire is located below high water marks. Again, these are areas where fire marks may be erased easily. Do not use stones from the stream for fireplace construction. Porous rocks may have enough moisture in them to form steam when heated. They could split with disastrous results.

Along with a match supply, tinder is the first requirement. Consider dry moss, match-sized sticks or twigs, or even knife whittled paper thin shavings as tinder. A fuzz stick is also useful. It basically is a partially-shaved stick with the shavings still attached. Make a mini-teepee, or wigwam of the kindling materials. At this point some lay on the whole fire from small to large before they ignite it. Others prefer to start the tinder burning and then lay on bits of slightly larger sticks, pyramiding them gradually. Larger sticks follow. A small camper's saw makes the handling of these larger sticks easier. To establish good burning of these larger pieces, try to place them loosely, exposing as much surface area as possible to the flames. The more surface area that can be exposed, the better the fire will take. Don't wedge them tightly together. The fire needs a good supply of air to take effectively.

Fireplace designs serve two functions: fire containment and support for your pan or backpacker's grill. There are any number of fireplace designs, but the two most common and useful seem to be the "U" shape and the keyhole. Both are built of rocks and are just what the names imply with regard to shape. The "U" has one end open for feeding in the wood while the back is closed off to reflect the heat forward. One layer of good sized rocks is sufficient. If no large rocks are readily available, smaller ones can be used, stacked two layers high. Don't worry about chinks or holes in such a wall: The cracks will help maintain a good supply of air to the fire. The keyhole is round at one end, and tapers to about a six-inch wide slot at the other end. It's a good functional design. The wood is burned in the center of the keyhole. As coals form, they are raked over into the keyhole slot, assuring that the cooking will not be subjected to the vagaries of leaping flames. The gathered coals provide an even, constant heat for the cooking.

In breaking camp, the fire must be out—absolutely, certainly, completely and unmistakeably out—drowned and drowned again. Test with your hands to be sure.

In truly soggy conditions when a fire is most desirable, it may take something even more persuasive than matches alone to get a fire going well. The first thought is often some stove fuel poured over wet wood. Generally, this simply tends to flare off without really igniting the wood. Better to search for a downed porous wood and thoroughly soak it in the stove fuel. Also, look for a good pitchy wood in a decomposing downed wood. Candle stubs are helpful fire starters in tough conditions. Others carry *Fire Ribbon*, a flammable paste which can be smeared thoroughly on wet wood (it's also used to prime gas or kerosene stoves), or any of the various solid fuel tablets.

Extra matches are essential in your pack. These backup match supplies must be protected from moisture. Some pack them in foil envelopes, plastic bags, or use the commercially available match boxes of plastic or metal. These latter boxes usually have their own striking surface.

# Food

There's a diversity of taste out there in the great American wilderness, and every conceivable viewpoint is in print. Authors appear quite knowledgable about the virtues of their views and, by God, they're sincere. I have read a couple of the arguments for foodstuffs that sound, at least to me, about as appetizing as munching on a well-soaked phone directory. This is not to say there isn't good advice available. It's just that I recommend you amble off to your local bookstore and examine the singular approaches that appeal to you. They're there, all neatly lined up, from the roots and herbs coterie to those who can give you the exact proportions of fats, proteins, and carbohydrates in just about any edible item grown on this little planet. Also there are a few belt-busting gourmands around who apparently eat anything as long as there is enough of it. They stop just short of recommending a pack mule move your entire kitchen into the boondocks.

Given this background, we will tread lightly on what you should eat and give mention to the resources available and the considerations involved with ultimately getting that "something" into your stomach.

The novice backpacker is advised to undertake a couple of short shakedown trips before setting out on any extended trek. Not only is this an opportunity to translate theory into experience, but any minor equipment problems or deficiencies can be understood and remedied. A further advantage is that you can rely primarily, if not entirely, on items from the supermarket. Other equipment needs for a couple days of travel should not be excessive, so food weight and preservation are not the problems they would be on a longer, more involved trip. This enables planning meals that are fairly close to your established, at-home, eating habits. Many find a drastic alteration in eating habits is not only a problem to the taste buds but the entire system as well. These shakedowns also provide an insight to developing on-trail eating requirements. Many, but by no means all, find their appetites greatly increased with additional activity, especially if the most recent exertions have consisted of chasing the secretary around the water cooler. The normal daily recommendation to satisfy trail appetites is between 4000 and 5000 calories. Covering several miles a day over varied terrain with a moderately heavy pack is a good day's work and makes some definite energy demands that must be replenished by the food carried in your pack.

This same message came across to me in a different light some time ago in the northern interior of British Columbia. Traveling with a great old river rat named Jim who was as familiar with the area as most people are with their shoe size, he brought an approach to most things that was about as subtle as a trash compactor. I'd spent the morning after grayling and rainbows in the river and finally realized I was getting hungry. Knowing Jim insisted on punctuality, I was relieved to see him fussing about the cook fire when I finally got back to camp. Approaching him I said, "Jim, my man, that smells good and looks good." He looked up briefly and snapped, "Dammit lad, ya' betta' like it. There ain't no McDonalds out here ya' know."

The first source of trail food selection is the supermarket with any number of items that may be repackaged for individual servings as well as a host of dehydrated and instant foods, soups, mixes, desserts and hot and cold drink offerings. The latest entry in convenience offerings comes from the freeze-dried process. This vacuum sublimation process is expensive and complex, so the final product costs are comparatively high. There are compensations: weight and space saving, and a long shelf life. There is rapid rehydration and generally there is no cooking involved (just add the hot or cold water and wait five or ten minutes). This process also permits the product to retain a great deal of the original flavor and color of freshly prepared foods. A surprising variety is available to include many meat and dairy products which have traditionally offered preservation problems. An overall consensus from most hikers is that freeze dried items are surprisingly good.

There is normally some at-home preparation before taking to the trail. A few items may go directly into the pack but most foods are usually repackaged. Measure out each meal and place it in a separate, labeled plastic bag. Any

*Modern freeze-dried foods are available in a staggering variety. They provide weight and space saving advantages for the backpacker. Freeze-dried foods rehydrate rapidly and are easy to prepare.*

required cooking directions should be torn from the original container and inserted with the ingredients. Some leave it at this, others take it a step further. For example, set all the makings of similar meals in small plastic bags, then place them together in a larger labeled bag. The result is all breakfast meals are together in a large bag, all lunches in another and all dinners in still another large bag. Some juggle by trail days: placing the Saturday menu of breakfast, lunch, and dinner in their small individual bags; then placing them in a larger labeled bag. Each day is subsequently set aside in a similar manner.

Once in the woods most follow a routine of breakfast, midmorning trail snack, lunch, midafternoon snack and dinner. Often a light snack or hot drink will be taken just before retiring. Others seem to like a routine of breakfast followed by more or less continual nibbling all day until the evening meal. A usual practice after breakfast is to get out that day's lunch or lunch and dinner, and place them conveniently high in the pack for easy access at the next stop. Lunches tend to be simple and light and usually cold, although some do like to fire up the stove briefly for soups or hot drinks. Evening meals are usually hot, and should be the most substantial meal of the day.

In addition to the standard trial menu and trail snacks appropriate to the trip, everyone should carry an emergency food ration. The main requirement is a choice that will keep well for a long time. With the light weight and convenience of various soup and hot drink packets, both cold and hot items are

52

available in any emergency ration. The final selection should be foil wrapped, placed in a plastic bag, sealed or taped tightly and placed in the bottom of the pack. Depending on the selection, either eat the contents once a year or throw them out and replace them on an annual basis.

A trail menu should be fairly light, pack well, offer a good variety, and be easy to prepare. It should also taste reasonably good, be easy to digest, be good to your system, and provide sound nutritional value. The judicious selection of standard supermarket items, dehydrated and instant foods plus freeze dried selection (possibly supplemented by any individual preferences met by specialty health, ethnic, or gourmet stores) allows us to eat well at reasonable cost.

Once again I recommend you check various books devoted exclusively to food selection and trail menus. Most of the manufacturers of freeze dried items also have available information on menu planning and meal preparation. There is also one book which I'd suggest you look into. This is *The Sportsmedicine Book* by Gabe Mirkin, M.D. and Marshall Hoffman (Little, Brown & Co.; Boston/Toronto, 1978 First Edition). The specific sections that relate directly to this chapter involve how the muscles work, what you should eat, and information about vitamins and minerals. You'll find some valuable information that occasionally offers a new insight or viewpoint from some of the established traditions.

Somehow this fairly simple, albeit important, business of getting something into the stomach assumes the significance of a religious conversion. Or, it can be fairly casual. I'd waded ashore from the Little Red River in Arkansas when I hailed a passing hiker. We sat together for lunch and talked for quite a while, mostly about the fishing. While I munched on a sandwich, he pulled a great green plastic bag from his pack, which held the contents of about eight boxes of wheat crackers. After he'd eaten a bunch of them, I asked if this was the only food he was carrying? He grinned and said, "Oh hell no. You should see the oatmeal I've got."

If you like it and it keeps you going—eat it.

# 9.

# CLOTHING

Proper clothing can make the difference between a comfortable trip and an uncomfortable one. Indeed, the difference may conceivably be survival itself. Extreme? Not really. There are just too many well-documented instances of serious trouble resulting from hikers encountering conditions for which they weren't prepared. This isn't just a regional problem. Western mountains are high enough that even packers with a minimum of experience should sense the potential for change in the high country. Eastern mountains are comparatively low but they are not to be underestimated. They too may brew up some vicious weather on short notice. Mt. Washington in New Hampshire is famed for its abrupt and severe weather changes, but a similar, if somewhat less extreme, situation exists in most areas that would be of concern to the angler-packer.

If there is a basic danger to avoid, it lies in being underequipped for potential weather changes. Oddly enough, even though clothing is so important, the new backpacker probably owns most of what would go along on a typical trek. There are no set standards because everyone seems to work out their own useful combinations. The most universal agreement we might expect from experienced hikers is a basic adherence to the principle of layered clothing.

On a seasonal basis, summer conditions are the easiest to cope with. Both shorts and long pants are common sights along the trail, but shorts are cooler and more comfortable. Cargo pockets mounted low enough to reach into them easily when the hip belt of the pack is tightened are a plus. Long pants may be included in the pack. They are certainly welcomed if you have to tromp through underbrush, especially with briars and biting insects. Plain cotton or cotton/synthetic blends are comfortable. Many find satisfaction with army surplus fatigues. They are tightly woven, durable, loosely cut, and fairly quick drying. In most trout country travel, don't discount the virtue of wool pants. Cool wet weather may come up at any time. Cotton loses its insulation value rapidly whereas wool continues to provide good insulation. In spring and fall wool pants are a must. They must be considered a summer essential for many areas as well.

Tee shirts, tank tops, and fishnet shirts are seen regularly along summer trails, although a lightweight, long-sleeved, cotton shirt is usually ideal. The sleeves may be rolled up or down depending on temperatures and insect populations. My standard is an old Orvis fishing shirt which looks a bit weary now but continues to wear well. On marginal days it's especially good over a fishnet shirt. The fishnets provide a means of heat regulation. If the outer shirt is opened to the breezes, the gaps in the fishnet permit the air to reach your skin. If the outer shirt is buttoned or zipped, the trapped air is an insulating, warming layer. In selecting fishnets, look for closely woven fabric at the shoulder. Otherwise the pack straps will ultimately drive the netting into your skin. It doesn't sound like too much of a deal, but packs do get heavy and your shoulders can become needlessly and surprisingly sore.

*Ace Manley (left) and Tony Skilton (right) compare notes. Their Orvis* Fishing *Shirts are excellent for the backpacker. Comfortable on the trail, they feature four front flapped pockets, a sunglass pocket on the sleeve, and a large cargo back pocket. Ample capacity for the flies and small accessories needed on a typical trip.*

With falling temperatures it's time to reach into the pack for additional help. There are several possibilities, either singly or in combination: wool shirts, sweaters, insulated vests, and jackets. Sweaters that button or zip down the front may be preferable to pullovers. This arrangement offers better warming-cooling potential. A pullover is either on or it's off and back in the pack. On those questionable days this is a nuisance.

What else? Well, a lightweight waterproof shell garment may be handy over shirts, sweaters, or insulated jackets. A lightweight, nylon, wind shirt weighs very little and contributes nicely to effective layering. A light, broad-brimmed hat is helpful for eye relief in most areas and keeps the rain from trickling down the back of your neck. Even in deep-woods walking, the brim may be soaked with repellent to contend with the arrival of deer flies and other assorted insect pests. Most hikers carry a bandana or two and find multiple uses for them. Polarized glasses may be helpful. Most trout fishermen tend to prefer those with tan or amber lenses for both the eye relief offered and superior contrast enhancement. Another hat, this time of wool, and your choice of gloves or mittens might be useful for cold nights. The head and the hands radiate away a great deal of heat.

The real clothing concern is balance through effective layering. The versatility to meet and adjust rapidly to changing temperatures is best done through layering lighter garments as opposed to selecting a single, thicker item.

The last routine consideration is rain protection. Depending on the prevailing temperatures, severity of the rain, and the individual hiker's attitude, rain may be handled in various ways. If it has been hot and humid, rain may be welcomed. Many just continue to walk wet. There are alternatives, one of which is the packboard poncho. Essentially this is a big rectangle of coated nylon with a hole for the head equipped with a hood. It is cut roomy enough to encompass both the pack and the packer. Even with a poncho legs will still get wet. Some hikers add rain chaps or full rain pants for additional protection. Many like gaiters as well when the going is wet and sloppy. Finally, there are those who ignore all of the foregoing and prefer to pitch a tarp and wait the weather out in relative comfort.

The total question of waterproof clothing has always been somewhat of a problem. When moisture can't get in, it can't get out. New materials are said to provide one way waterproofing. That is, they exhibit the ability to keep rain out but permit body moisture to escape. These materials are *Bukflex*® and *Gore-Tex*®. *Bukflex* has been around a bit longer and many users report satisfaction. The new *Gore-Tex* is generating a great deal of interest with applications showing up not only in clothing but sleeping bags and tents as well. It isn't cheap. However, discussions about *Gore-Tex* with a few individual users and various industry sources show that enthusiasm is running high. There will be more and more offerings available. Look them over. Perhaps there will be something here for you.

The three seasons of probable activity offer such a variety of climatic conditions that sensible clothing selection is absolutely vital to the comfort and safety of any trip. Manufacturers do a fine job of providing the clothing that can meet any climatic requirement. It's up to you to realistically consider your needs for comfort and weather protection. Examine the offerings with the intended uses of each item uppermost in mind. If you select wisely, comfort and weather protection will never be a problem.

# 10.

# THE CAMP SITE

There are natural rhythms to trail life. Active and energetic days begin to wind down towards rest and relaxation as camp sites are selected and prepared. On the surface a camp is a utilitarian haven providing comfort, convenience, and renewal. Between old-time trail companions it is this and more. Camps previously shared become reference points for subliminal reservoirs of memory. Even the most casual reminders are enough to ripple their surface. "remember when we set up camp near the West Branch?" "How 'bout the time the raccoon came into camp up on Slide Mountain?" Distant memories become selective and self-serving as a flood of imagery comes to the eye of the mind through past trips recalled and relived.

A good camp is an important part of the overall trail experience; its location is a definite consideration in the daily routine. Normal planning should include the daily distance to be covered and an estimate of where the night will be spent. Enough trail time should be allotted to reach your destination well before sundown. This allows ample time for specific site selection, setting up camp, cooking, and clean up. These early set-ups are especially appreciated if your evening plans call for some time on nearby streams or lakes.

There are two types of camps: the brief overnight setup and the established base camp for a longer stay. The longer the stay in one location, the greater the environmental impact will be. Any site should provide convenience, safety, and protection from the full force of the elements. It should also be sanitary and environmentally sound.

In well-traveled areas there are obviously established sites of past occupancy. If they are empty and well-located, they should be utilized. Otherwise, a new location should be found. Although the casual evidence of unfortunately popular areas might suggest the opposite, most backpackers prefer a measure of seclusion. Relative privacy is, after all, a part of the wilderness experience. The better sites are not chiseled out of the area. A well-drained, level site is optimal for sleeping comfort. Try lying down to double-check the area for levelness and suitability. Only large sticks and rocks that interfere with comfort should be removed from your selected area. If a very slight slope is absolutely unavoidable, sleep with your head higher than your feet. The forest duff (that accumulation of decaying leaves, decomposing twigs, bark, and needles) is probably the best sleeping surface. Other alternatives include sand, rocky soils, and bare ground. Never set up camp over vegetation if there is any other alternative. The former practice of digging drainage ditches or moats is no longer *de rigueur*; nor is it required with the modern tent on a well-drained surface.

The camp should be physically safe. Check for any overhead branches that may break and fall in a strong wind. If the area under consideration is backed by a high wall or cliff, walk back first and double-check for rocks that may become dislodged and roll dangerously close. Avoid dry washes, deep gullies, and ravines. They vary in intensity from being simply inconvenient if it rains during the night, to being subject to sudden flash flooding, sometimes from a storm in the mountains some distance away.

Although the modern tent provides excellent protection from the elements,

*he well-chosen campsite is convenient, sanitary, environmentally consider-* *te, safe and protected from the full force of the elements- a potential force that* *ust never be underestimated.*

59

a well-chosen site provides additional, natural protection. Large rocks, trees, and slight depressions of other natural cover minimize the effects of strong winds or driving rainstorms. In wet areas locate sites with mild breezes. Mosquitoes have difficulty with moving air currents. There is a normal reversal of air currents in mountainous country. Day breezes tend to move upslope during the day and downslope at night. Cool, damp, night air has a tendency to settle in basins and pockets. If you are able to find a level site part way up a hill, it will be several degrees warmer. Check the site for an eastern exposure for early morning sun.

A standard rule of thumb has been to camp at least 100 feet from a water source. In recent years this recommendation has been altered to at least 200 feet. An established base camp should invariably be located within easy striking distance of water. Generally, the overnight stop is similarly sited, although it is not quite as essential. If your map indicates there will be no water source near your planned overnight stop, water carriers can be filled at the last source available in the afternoon and carried to the proposed site.

If you will be using fire for cooking or aesthetic purposes, be sure to clear an appropriate area, say a ten foot circle, down to bare earth, and locate it safely away from the tent or other equipment. An ample supply of down and dead wood is also necessary for a fire.

Don't forget to find a latrine area. A simple overnight stop may only necessitate that you get well away from any trail, water source, or camp. Choose an area that no following group would ever be likely to select as a possible camp site. With a backpacker's trowel, try to remove a sod clump and loose soil to a depth of six to eight inches. Most hikers burn the toilet paper (but don't burn up the woods!). Cover the area with the loose soil and sod clump. If there is a base camp or a larger group, a more formal latrine area is called for. The latrine is made longer, since bacterial action and normal decomposition is greatest in the upper few inches of soil, greater depth is not needed. Each person agrees to use the same end and progressively fill in the area for obvious reasons of sanitation and insect control. Needless to say, this area is also selected for its general lack of character, well away from camp, trail, or water where no following group would be likely to want to locate a camp.

In breaking camp, take the time to check the area thoroughly for any scrap of paper or plastic. If there was a fire make sure that it is completely out. With a modicum of common sense and environmental concern, camp sites will be well located and safe and will properly contribute to the overall enjoyment of the trail experience.

# 11.

# MAP AND COMPASS

## Map

The standard navigational aids for the backpacker are the topographic map and compass. Depending on where you are traveling, there may be other maps that are valuable. Some of these possibilities include offerings from various state agencies, The Bureau of Land Management, The National Park Service, and the U.S. Forest Service. As a rule these latter maps are less detailed than topographic maps that cover the same area, but they may have the advantage of being more up to date with reagrd to trails and road systems.

Local topographic maps are in stock at your nearby outfitting shop and may also be carried by some general sporting goods outlets and book stores. They can also be obtained by mail. For areas east of the Mississippi River write:

Branch of Distribution
U.S. Geological Survey
1200 South Eads St.
Arlington, Virginia 22202

'or areas west of the Mississippi write:

Branch of Distribution
U.S. Geological Survey
Box 28286, Federal Center
Denver, Colorado 80225

Request a Topographic Map Index of the state you are interested in. You will receive an indexed map of the entire state divided into rectangles by a gridlike overlay. Each map covers a specific area of the state and is designated by name so you can easily determine the maps necessary for your planned travel. There is also an order form included. Standard quadrangle maps published in the $7\frac{1}{2}$ or 15 minute series are currently priced at $1.25.

The topo maps appropriate to the backpacker come in two series, 15 minute and 7.5 minute. The 15 minute series is excellent, covering a larger area than the 7.5 series but still providing sufficient detail. In some cases the 15 minute series may not be available: They are being gradually phased out in favor of the 7.5 series maps. These show great detail but cover a smaller area. Thus, you may require more maps to adequately cover your travels.

One term, "map scale," sometimes confuses new map readers. Map scale simply defines the relationship between the measurements of the features as shown on the map and as they exist on the earth's surface. This "scale" is normally stated as a ratio or a fraction: 1:24,000 or 1/24,000. Therefore the scale 1:24,000 says that any unit, such as 1 inch on the map represents 24,000 of the same unit on the ground.

The basic data for the two maps of most interest to us are:

| Series | Scale | One Inch Represents | Quandrangle Size— Lattitude & Longitude | Quadrangle Area Square Miles |
|---|---|---|---|---|
| 7.5 minute | 1:24,000 | 2000 feet | 7.5 × 7.5 Min. | 49 to 71 |
| 15 minute | 1:62,500 | about 1 mile | 15 × 15 Min. | 197 to 282 |

The 15 minute series with its "about an inch to the mile" ratio is very easy to work with in the field. Usually the 7.5 minute series with its inch equal to 2000 feet is roughly translated to a ratio of $2\frac{1}{2}$ inches to the mile.

Another valuable ally in this information quest is the:

National Cartographic Information Center
U.S. Geological Survey
507 National Center
Reston, Virginia 22092

They provide a national information service on maps, charts, aerial and space photographs, geodetic control and other cartographic data for the United States. They can inform you what data is available, identify which agency holds the data, and provide appropriate ordering information. One item, indispensable to the new backpacker, is their booklet: *Topographic Maps*. It explains everything you will ever need to know about reading and interpreting topographic symbols in a compact 27 page booklet. Some of the other specific materials they can provide are: a booklet, *Types of Maps Published by Govern ment Agencies*; a brochure with Field Offices of the Forest Service; a brochure, *The National Forests*; and several pages stapled together that provide various State Information Sources.

Excellent Canadian information is also available by mail. Contact:

> Dept. of Energy, Mines and Resources
> 615 Booth St.
> Ottawa, Ontario, Canadia K1A 0E9

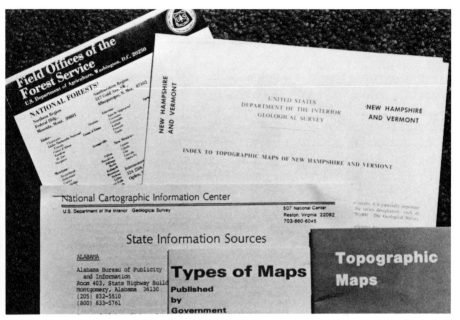

*The National Cartographic Information Center can be an important informa-tion source for the backpacker. Especially valuable may be their booklet,* Topographic Maps.

# Compass

There are various types of compasses available. Backpackers generally choose the orienteering models. Most of these are made by two companies, Silva and Suunto. Each company provides excellent products which range from basic, but eminently useful models, up to very precise and versatile models. The compass helps you place the map in the right position so the map's north and the world's north coincide. The compass also helps you read the land from the topographic map with required precision.

The basic compass is a circle divided into 360°. 0° is north, then following clockwise, 90° is east, 180° south, 270° west and 360° north. Note that 0° and 360° are the same. Defining a direction is done numerically, which is much easier than attempting a word definition. The magnetized needle points to an area defined as the magnetic North Pole, rather than the true geographic North Pole. The magnetic North Pole is approximately 1400 miles away from the true North Pole and is located on Bathurst Island.

Next, the magnetized needle moves on a pivot inside a fluid-filled round chamber. The end that indicates magnetic north is specially indicated, usually with red paint. The compass housing rim carries the initials of the cardinal points, north, east, south and west, On the Silva models each space between the lines on the housing represents two degrees. Each twentieth degree line is numerically marked (i.e., 20, 40, 60 and so on to 360 or N). The inside bottom

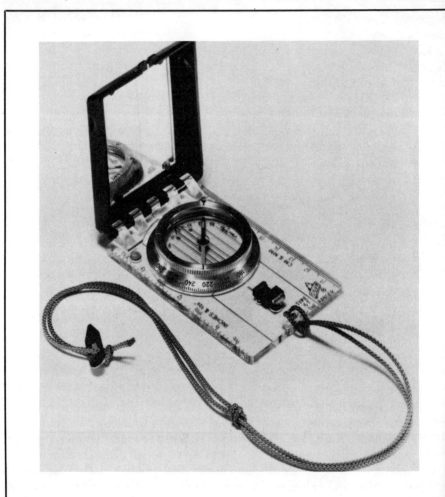

*The Silva* Ranger TD *features a sight and mirror allowing simultaneou observation of an object and the compass needle. The see-through housing ha an arrangement for declination adjustment.*

of the liquid-filled chamber is marked with an arrow, called the orienting arrow. There are parallel lines on either side of this arrow which are known as orienting lines. The compass is oriented when the north marking of the magnetized needle lies over the orienting arrow, pointing toward the letter N on the housing rim.

The compass housing turns readily and sits atop a rectangular transparent plastic base plate. A direction-of-travel line is marked in this base plate which runs from the housing rim toward the front edge of the base plate. This direction-of-travel arrow is also indicated back near the movable rim by engraved letters (read bearing here). The raised part of the base plate on which the compass housing will move has a black indexing pointer to show what degree number the compass housing is set at. Next, the side edges of the base plate are parallel to the direction-of-travel arrow. The front edge and a side edge have measuring markings. On the inexpensive *Polaris* the front is marked in inches, the side in millimeters. Some models have exchangeable scales for use with maps of different scales.

For average use a functional orienteering compass without a lot of extras is certainly adequate and quite inexpensive. The Silva *Polaris* is about $7.00, and the Silva *Explorer III* which is probably a bit easier to use with maps is less than $10.00. If there was extensive bushwhacking in trailess areas, I'd probably go with the Silva *Ranger 15TD*. Currently this lists in the $35 to $36.00 range. This doesn't imply that other compasses aren't as capable, but that the *Ranger 15TD* is a very versatile and precise instrument.

When purchasing any compass, take a few moments to compare it with others in stock to be sure the needle points in just the same direction. Rarely, but possibly, a needle will be misaligned or become stuck in a false position. Also keep it away from metal which may confuse and distort a reading.

Although we normally think in terms of map and compass together, there are some basic uses for which a compass is sufficient. It can find a direction or bearing, allow you to follow this bearing accurately, and return you to the original starting point.

With the orienteering compass, locating a bearing is straightforward. Face the destination, hold the compass at or above waist level with the direction-of-travel arrow pointing straight at the destination. Orient the compass by turning the housing (the housing only, not the baseplate) until the needle lies over the orienting arrow on the bottom of the compass housing, with its north (red) end pointing to the letter "N" on the rim. Now, read the bearing on the housing rim where the black index line aligns with the red direction-of-travel arrow on the base plate.

In the field let's assume you're standing on a slight hill or rise and can see a small pond off in the distance. Face the pond, hold the compass so that the direction-of-travel arrow points toward the pond. Rotate the compass housing until the red north arrow points toward "N" on the housing rim. Assume the bearing to be 140° and proceed straight toward the pond. But, as you come off the rise you lose sight of the pond and realize you won't be seeing it again until you reach its shores. Just repeat the original procedure, this time selecting a visible landmark such as a tree or rock that lies ahead in the correct direction of travel at 140°. Proceed to it, select another landmark ahead in the same line of travel, go to it and repeat this procedure as required until you arrive at the destination.

Return travel to the hill is just a half circle away or 180°. This back bearing can be done in two ways. The first procedure simply uses the orienteering compass in reverse. Going toward the pond, you had the arrow pointed away from you. It's possible to return by not resetting the compass at all. Just have the direction-of-travel arrow face you, hold it level, orient the compass by turning your body until the red north end again points to "N". Don't touch the compass housing at all, just sight across it (you'll see 320° facing you on the housing rim). Look up for a landmark, go to it and continue on in this manner until you reach your starting point on the hill. Or, perhaps more commonly, do it this way. Your outward course was 140°; add the half circle (180°) for a return bearing of 320°. If the original bearing was more than 180°, you would subtract. For instance, had you started from the pond toward the hill, your original bearing would have been 320°. To return to the pond you would subtract the 180° of a half circle for a bearing of 140°.

Although precision is the normal compass requirement, there may be occasions when introducing a deliberate bias or error is advantageous. The destination may be a small pond back in the woods. Let's say the pond is due north of your location. It's about two miles back in and there is no trail. However the map indicates a small outlet stream flowing to the east. Rather than attempt a due north course through the down timber and rough terrain, it would be easier to run a bearing a few degrees east of true north, knowing that you will intercept the outlet stream. Then, simply follow it upstream (west) to the source pond.

# Map and Compass

When the map and compass are used together, an important consideration is declination. The compass needle is responsive to magnetic north, not geographic north. The specific variation between the two is termed declination and is always given in the lower map margin. A vertical star-topped line indicates geographic north; the angle or slanted line topped by "MN" designates magnetic north. The angle between them is given numerically, advising you how many degrees east or west of geographic north to go to find magnetic north. The eastern states will show a declination west, the western states as well as much of the central and southern areas will show an easterly declination. Correcting for declination can be done by resetting the compass appropriately each time it is placed on the map. However, new map readers may occasionally forget, so there is an easier method of compensation. Simply correct the map in advance by providing declination lines which can't be ignored or forgotten

After adding the penciled-in declination lines, the map and compass can be made to speak the same language easily. Any compass setting made when these declination lines are used is valid without additional refiguring or compensation. The easiest way to prepare the map is to use a straight edge and pencil to draw a line across the map face in continuation of the magnetic north line on the lower map margin. Then, just as carefully, draw other lines parallel to this first line, spacing them an inch or so apart all across the map. Once this is done many hikers like to cover the map with a clear contact adhesive paper as protection against possible moisture in the field. Dampness won't bother the compass but a soggy map is difficult to deal with.

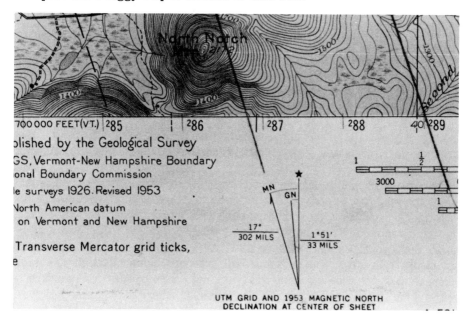

*The slanted line, topped by MN, indicates magnetic north and the number of degrees of variation from geographic north. Correct the map before use by adding penciled-in declination lines. Extend the declination line carefully, using a straightedge, so that it continues across the map face. Add parallel lines an inch or so apart across the entire map. Compensation for declination will be required for accurate travel.*

The first practice sessions with map and compass are best done in a familiar area. We must make the map and compass correspond to the lay of the land. With the declination lines drawn on your map you can orient the map and compass from the magnetic north diagram on the map or from one of the corresponding magnetic north lines you've added to the map face. Set the compass at 360°, (north, that is). The "N" mark on the housing rim is now aligned with the direction-of-travel arrow. Then place the compass on the map so the base plate side edge is parallel with the magnetic north line of the declination diagram. Now turn the map with the compass lying on top of it until the north (red) portion of the needle comes into agreement and points to the "N" mark of the compass rim. Everything is aligned now. The direction-of-travel arrow, the north end of the compass needle, and the orienting arrow on the bottom of the compass housing all point to magnetic north.

With the map correctly oriented, the direction between any two points on the map will be the same as the physical relationship between the same two points on the land. To travel from here to there, place the compass on the map with the edge of the base plate touching your starting point and your destination. The direction-of-travel arrow is heading toward where you want to go. The compass needle is pointing toward magnetic north. Now, turn the compass housing until the orienting arrow lies parallel to one of the magnetic north lines you have added to the map. Everything agrees: The red end of the needle lines up with the "N" mark on the housing rim and lies directly over the orienting arrow. Just look to where the black indexing pointer aligns with the direction-of-travel arrow for the bearing to follow.

Fold the map and pick up the pack. Hold the compass level and turn your body so everything agrees again. The needle is directly over the orienting arrow and points to the "N" of the housing rim. Select a landmark ahead of the direction-of-travel arrow, go to it, pick up another landmark and so on to your destination.

Locating your position on the map is also rather straightforward. As usual, orient the map and compass, rotating them together until the needles line up with the "N" marker of the compass rim. Find a prominent landmark on the map and locate the same point on the ground. Say a particular mountain is visible from your position. Aim the direction-of-travel arrow at the mountain and check its direction from your position. Draw or imagine a straight line from this peak. You are standing along this line. Find a second peak or landmark, get a careful bearing on it, draw or imagine this line. Where they intersect is your location. Sometimes fishermen on large lakes can use this procedure. If a reef or shoal has been located well out in the lake and it's a spot to which you'd like to return, look for prominent and permanent landmarks around the shore. These may be mountains, cliffs, or even islands. Make careful bearings on two such landmarks and mark the information on the map or in a notebook. For instance, you might make a note similar to this: "Submerged reef gave up excellent fishing at dawn, bearing 40° to the island, 320° to Eagle Mtn. peak."

If you stick mostly to well-marked and maintained trails you won't require much of the compass. Still, it is an item you want to have within easy reach. It's worth checking from time to time just to be sure of your bearings. If you know from your pre-trip planning that you should be heading mostly in an easterly direction and a quick check shows you're heading north, something is obviously wrong and needs correction.

In the final analysis there is no substitute for practice with a map and compass in hand. I really doubt that much is to be gained by reading a chapter about their use unless you go out and practice the methods. By all means

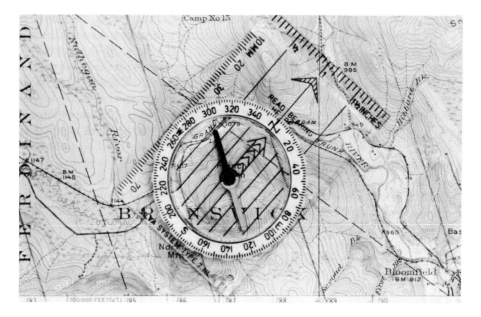

When the map is correctly oriented, place the compass on the map so the base plate edge connects your starting point and your destination.

Turn the compass housing until the orienting arrow is parallel to one of the declination lines you have added to the map. Everything comes to agreement. The red (N) end of the needle points to the N on the housing rim and lies directly over the orienting arrow. Just look to where the black index pointer aligns with direction-of-travel arrow for the bearing to follow (in this case 60°).

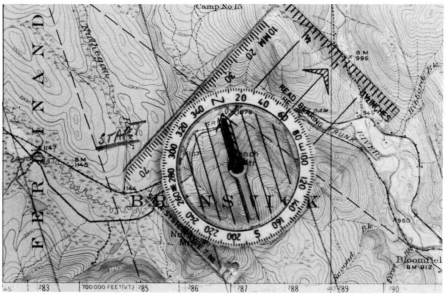

purchase a compass. For most uses an inexpensive, orienteering model will be satisfactory. At the same time get a local topographic map from your dealer and go out in the field and work with them. Be sure to realize the importance of declination and make the proper compensations for it. I'm told that a degree of compass error is something over 90 feet per mile. In an area with a large declination you could go pretty far astray in short order unless the proper compensation is made. Also, in some cases I've outlined what should be the easiest handling methods, but not the only handling methods, so thoroughly study the directions that come with the compass. It may even be well to read one of the many good books that deal with orienteering.

# 12.

# TROUT SENSES

In spite of a modest ranking on the evolutionary scale, trout are well-suited to their specialized environment and possess a number of keen sensory receptors which respond to a variety of impressions. Many anglers feel they are an ideal quarry; shy, cautious, and demanding of an angler's good effort if there is to be a degree of consistency in their capture.

The hearing of trout is an unusually versatile sensory system that is essential to their feeding and survival. This is a two part system, and yes, trout have ears (although they are internal, rather than external). Their hearing is aided by a connection between the swim bladder and the inner ear. Essentially the swim bladder is a membrane-enclosed chamber capable of serving as an underwater amplifier, microphone and resonating chamber. The bladder notices vibration which is magnified and transmitted to the inner ear. Trout also have lateral line sensitivity to vibration. The lateral line begins on the head as a canallike network. Behind the head canals join and form the true lateral line extending towards the tail. The two systems are complementary to the extent that the lateral line detects primarily near-field vibrations and the inner ear system is alert to more distant sounds. The systems are so sensitive that a nearby baitfish, worm or nymph may be detected without being seen. The systems hear various low frequency, auditory stimuli from about ten to fifteen cycles per second to some 10,000 cycles per second. In a comparative sense, the average human hears in the ranges of about twenty to 20,000 cycles per second.

Sound travels underwater at about one mile per second, a rate about five times the speed of travel in the air. Additionally, sound intensity is not decreased nearly so much as in the air, since water is an excellent sound wave conductor. Despite this, our talking back and forth above the surface will not alarm the trout to our presence. These air borne sounds are not easily transmitted into the water. The surface is a very effective barrier to most air borne sound formations. Although talking will not alarm the trout to our presence, we can easily alert them in other ways. Any object in contact with the water will easily transmit warning vibrational echoes. The angler should wade carefully, especially in quiet waters, and tread softly along bordering stream banks. In turbulent waters our presence may be muted by the sounds of the stream itself as it tumbles and cascades. For reasons of secure footing and personal safety, we should be cautious and slow moving in the rapids.

The olfactory senses are also well developed. Two nostrils are arranged as U-shaped tubes in the snout of the fish. Water passing through the tubes flows over highly sensitive nerve endings. This system is so sensitive that it can detect some odors diluted into the incredible ratios of parts per billion. It can, for instance, detect the odor of other nearby fish and make distinctions between them. A crippled bait fish giving off an alarm substance as its distress may be checked out quickly in the hope of obtaining an easy meal. Perhaps we should confirm the suspected: Sensory systems work in conjunction with one another. Our theoretically crippled, fluttering bait fish may be detected by odor, by sight, or it may be detected through vibrational echoes set up by its struggles. The underlying point remains the same: Trout are keenly aware of what is happening around them.

Some of the various odors that have been found to deter or frighten trout include human skin, insect repellents, and various petroleum-based products. In an attempt to counteract these considerations, there are various scents offered by some manufacturers for application to flies and lures. Whether these offerings actually have the ability to attract trout or simply achieve an effect of masking human odors is a consideration I've never analyzed. However, given the olfactory sensitivity of the trout plus the demonstrated success of chumming, stink baits, etc. for other species, it is reasonable to assume that scent could be an attractor element in many circumstances, especially in turbid waters when normal keen vision of the trout is greatly hampered. I recall a conversation over a Colorado campfire when one of the group smeared bacon fat over his Marabou Muddler, assuring me, "It works like a charm."

There is an obvious relationship between odor discrimination and taste. Trout have taste buds on the inside of their mouths. Unfortunately, some taste buds exist outside the mouth as well. This means a trout can actually taste something without taking it into its mouth. The occasional gentle bump to a fly or lure may indicate an attempt to taste the object before actually striking.

Vision is another extremely important sensory capacity, and their ability to accurately define and intercept drifting nymphs and flies is reliable proof of their capabilities.

In spite of the obvious environmental differences, the lidless eye of the trout is surprisingly like our own basic structure. The retina's sensor lining includes both rods and cones. Rods permit light-sensing functions in marginal and very low level illuminations, while the cones are color sensitive and function in ordinary daylight levels. As the light levels diminish into darkness the rod cells are utilized, permitting the trout to still see well, especially in terms of size and silhouette. They appear to retain a degree of tonal value discrimination at night even if color vision is absent. Many hatches occur in the darkness and are silhouetted against the night sky. The most successful anglers attempt to reasonably suggest the size, shape, and tonal values of the natural insect. If the essential values are light in color, the artificial should also be light in color; if dark values predominate, the artificial should be correspondingly dark. Imitative precision may not be required but reasonable approximation is still advantageous. Well in advance of dawn the cones begin extending in anticipation of daylight, and the trout evidences excellent abilities in the areas of color perception and shape discrimination.

Since water is a lesser conductor of light than air, the trout have little need for long range vision and are primarily nearsighted. As their eyes are placed on the sides of the head they have a very wide field of sight and they are able to use their eyes independently or together.

Used independently, each eye is able to scan an area of about 180°. When both eyes are focused on a subject, the field of view is rather narrow. Most authorities indicate 45° as the likely field of view. Because of the location of their eyes, trout have a small blind spot directly below and behind themselves.

Their ability to see above the surface is affected by and related to the physical properties of light. As light rays pass from the air to the water they are bent or refracted. The degree of refraction is proportional to the angle at which the light rays strike the surface. Light rays that are perpendicular to the surface are not bent, while those rays entering nearly parallel to the surface are refracted at an angle of 48.5°. Because light may enter the surface from all directions, the trout can see all objects above the surface. However light rays are bent as they enter the water and funnel into a conelike shape having an apical angle of 97°. The narrow base of the cone leads up to the window or circular hole in the surface. The trout's view through the window shows objects in the center area of the window most clearly, while items at the edges of the window are blurred and compressed. Their single view to the outside world is through this window. The remainder of the underside of the surface becomes mirrorlike, bouncing back the light and forming an image of the bottom.

Close approaches to visible trout, especially in slow flowing or calm, clear water are best accomplished by crouching to remain low, towards the edges of the window where any image seen by the trout may be indistinct and compressed. In addition to bending low, side arm casts are often the most advantageous offering with close approaches. Kneeling and crawling tactics can be helpful, and bank-bound anglers should take advantage of boulders, brush, and other cover to break up and confuse their outlines.

The exact size of the trout's window varies with the depth of the fish. At about six inches beneath the surface the window is approximately a foot. The fish most interested in near-surface and surface activity often hold some six to eighteen inches beneath the surface with their attention concentrated upward. Any deep-lying fish have a proportionately larger window to the world but they are more apt to be concentrating their attention on deep lying or deep drifting food forms.

Anglers often question why a trout should take an artifical fly at all, especially when the hook appendage is so obvious. It is a question of vexing specificity. Although we cannot know the total answer, we gain partial insight by realizing that although their eyes detect color, size, form, motion perception and contrast, the eyes of the trout provide a comparatively lesser capacity for exact detail. Their ability to see sharply is best when an object is at right angles to their eyes. They sacrifice some detail for depth perception enhancement when they look straight ahead and snap at a fly. In effect, a sense of familiar, recognizable "insectness" at this critical moment, rather than each specific detail is what is being zeroed in on. The more important triggering mechanisms are size, shape or silhouette, color (though not necessarily exact shading) and movement, or equally important, lack of movement. Some of the swirling last minute refusals we experience may result from unusual behavioral characteristics.

A natural may fly will drift freely with the vargaries of an existing current while our artificial fly, attached to a leader, may become subject to unnatural motion or drag. Although drag is often anticipated or detected by the angler and compensated for, some movement is so subtle as to be invisible to the angler. The trout, just inches away, is the definitive judge of such things. Active insects fluttering or struggling on the surface film may be suggested by subtle twitches delivered through a sensitive rod hand. On a few occasions movement is advantageous even when the natural flies are drifting motionless. Such moments might occur when a hatch is particularly heavy and your offering is just one of thousands available. We experienced such moments in the Labrador interior when mayfly emergences on the shallow lakes were enormous. Brook trout to seven pounds were gulping in the naturals with abandon. It seemed pure chance that our single artificial could be found in the midst of such activity. When we began to skitter our offerings, the movement caught the eye of the heavy trout. They would move consistently to our gently twitched offerings.

In addition to behavior, and certainly as important on a day-to-day basis, are the size and silhouette of our offerings. They may be close enough to bring an investigative arousal but not quite close enough to finish the job. Matching size becomes increasingly important as the fly becomes smaller in size. A suggestively lifelike appearance becomes more important as the currents slow. In the slower flows the trout have infinitely more time to spiral up and inspect the drifting fly, for the current won't wash it rapidly away. In quick, turbulent flows a more reflexive attack is required as the potential food form would be quickly lost to the current. This strongly suggests that during emergence activity the angler pay more attention to size, shape, color and manner of movement in slow to medium currents than would be required in tumbling, cascading flows. Actually, if trout were capable of expressing emotion, we'd probably find these last minute refusals were as disappointing to them as they are to us (although we usually suspect otherwise). Their daily well-being is a constant battle between expended energy and the capture of an adequate food supply. They investigate, hoping to reinforce their initial impression of the correct "insectness" and behavior of our offerings.

In turbid, vision-hindered water, trout must depend heavily on their unusual lateral line sensitivity and sense of smell for much of their food location. Many anglers respond to such water conditions by selecting somewhat larger than normal flies in tonal values that enhance contrast. If fishing subsurface, which is the norm under such conditions, tinsel-ribbed flies reflect any available light values as the trout moves in close. Fly patterns such as the Muddler and, of course, various spin lures may set up vibrational echoes that stimulate lateral line sensitivity and aid in locating the offering in such discolored water conditions. Fishing the water more slowly and more thoroughly is also productive for any prey must be accurately located before the trout can strike. In milky waters that prevail on some limestone streams and snow-melt waters, as well as those coffee brown runoff waters, large dark flies are often employed for contrast enhancement.

In normal conditions of seasonal water levels and clear water, if you're stuck for a subsurface starting point, select a fly corresponding to the stream bottom values. Nature protects the otherwise defenseless nymphs and larva primarily through protective coloration. They usually blend in well with their surroundings. A dislodged or drifting nymph under these clear water conditions doesn't require contrast enhancement. The trout's eye is very sensitive to movement and they expect to see something appropriate to the locale.

The ability of trout to select is another, much discussed, consideration. Obviously the ability exists and is of great value to the well being of the trout. Over the long haul the trout is an opportunistic feeder, snapping at what is available within the confines of a rubble foundation and moving, liquid roof to his world. However, when an emergence of an insect species begins, there is an entirely different situation. Thousands of a similar species become available, all moving in a similar manner, all of a similar size, shape and appropriate color. The trout becomes quite specific in its feeding habit in order to make maximum utilization of this temporary abundance. By selecting a site in the flow where the current brings a constant drift line of insects, the trout is able to initiate and repeat a muscular movement of great efficiency, intercepting the drifting insect, then returning to precisely the same spot (by fixing a specific location on the retina) to lie in wait for another insect before repeating the same muscular pattern. This is certainly the most efficient way to utilize this transitory abundance.

The artifical offered at such a time should be of a similar size, silhouette, color and manner of movement as the natural. The best presentation is the natural drift line of the insects that the specific trout is intercepting. The trout certainly won't move a foot to one side to take your artifical when it is in the feeding rhythm of picking the naturals off overhead.

Selectivity is at once a strength and a potential Achilles heel for the angler.

All we have to do is put the right fly in the right place.

Many fertile waters have times when two, three, or more insect species are emerging simultaneously. It's critical to determine not only which insect your trout is taking, but the developmental state of the insect as well. Numerical abundance or relative ease of capture may be the influencing factors determining which stage and which insect the trout is feeding on. Careful observation of the hatch is most important. There may be a small, darkly colored species available in vast numbers which are difficult to see while you concentrate your imitative efforts on a more visible species which the trout are ignoring at the moment. Under difficult lighting conditions or on large streams, a small pair of binoculars can be surprisingly useful. You can visually locate and follow a particular fly to determine its fate. Later, when the specific hatches are over, some trout may begin to cruise, searching for any leftovers from the hatch, or they may show susceptibility to other offerings in an opportunistic manner.

In spite of their voracious feeding during specific hatches, they are often strangely cautious with the arrival of a new food form on the scene. Most hatches run their course in a week or ten days to be replaced by another species attaining numerical superiority. Yet there seems to be a recognition factor at work and an initial reluctance to change to the new insect form. On the upper section of a river that I fish regularly, the arrival of *Ephemerella dorothea* (locally Pale Evening Duns or Sulphurs) is well regarded and capable of providing good activity. Surprisingly, the first day or two that we notice some emergence activity, the trout ignore the little flies and prefer instead larger, darker, spinner patterns that have been the standard offerings for the past several evenings. By the third day the trout seem to have reconciled any early recognition problems and feed avidly on the buttery yellow little flies. On this same stream section we also see a few, but very few, *Ephemera varia* (locally: Yellow Drake) emerge. Trout in this section ignore them even though they are large and drift placidly for long distances on the slow-flowing current. We've often watched naturals drift a hundred yards or more through feeding trout and not be taken. Yet thirty miles downriver where the steam is considerably larger and population levels of *E. varia* are considerably higher, this is an eagerly awaited emergence. Large trout rise well to their appearance.

Still another consideration directly affecting the trout is water temperature. Since trout are cold-blooded, their body temperatures are those of the surrounding waters. This heat transfer process speeds up or slows down the metabolic processes. Consequently, water temperatures have a direct bearing on reproduction, feeding, growth and survival.

Their sensitivity to temperature changes is such that they are capable of detecting differences of less than half a degree. Such sensitivity has many applications. Sea run trout and salmon supplement their keen sense of smell when migrating along a thermal current enroute to distant feeding grounds or returning to their home rivers. It is also fundamental to their ability to locate spring holes, cold water seepages, and cooling tributaries in times of distressingly high water temperatures in the main body of water.

Angling results are often directly affected by water temperature. Trout will feed all year round; however, metabolic functions are greatly slowed in the cold water of winter. Food taken in may require four to five days or more to be fully digested, so the length of time between stomach refills is greatly lengthened.

*As waters warm beyond comfortable limits, trout often seek out riffly or rapid areas, spring hole seepages, or cooling tributaries in search of higher oxygen contents and/or cooler temperatures.*

As water temperatures rise, trout require more food more often, as their body processes are greatly accelerated. More energy is being used. They are increasingly active and digestive times are greatly shortened. Most authorities conclude that maximum trout growth occurs between 45° and 66° although trout can and do feed above and below these benchmarks.

Fly fishermen who have charted their results in relation to prevailing water temperatures tend to prefer a reasonably narrow range, from about 55° to 68°. At 68° and warmer the availability of insect activity to stimulate feeding seems to become more and more important. With warming temperatures it is much more difficult to simply pound up a trout by thoroughly covering the water. Additional stimulation in the form of insect activity greatly enhances the prospects of success at such times.

When waters warm above comfortable limits, the trout tend to search out rapid waters. If temperatures climb toward the mid seventies, they often concentrate in cool tributaries or spring hole seepages. At these temperatures trout may be distressed either because of water temperatures or insufficient oxygen contents in the water. During these periods you can often find cooler, more desirable temperatures upstream, near the stream source, or in various tributary streams. Trout gravitate toward cooler areas. Surprisingly large trout are sometimes found in such cool, sheltered areas. Some regions have cold water releases on rivers that have been impounded for water supply use or hydroelectric power generation. Water released to the rivers from the bottom of such impoundments flow cool and may exert an influence for several miles on the main stream.

Because of the direct relationships of temperature and trout activity, many anglers habitually carry a small stream thermometer. Move a reasonable distance into the stream, shade the thermometer from the direct sun, and hold it beneath the surface long enough for it to register a consistent reading. On ponds and lakes the same situation applies. Many anglers tie the thermometer to a length of monofilament or discarded fly line section so they can lower it deep in a search for spring holes or cold water seepages.

Throughout the most desirable temperature ranges, digestion may take twelve hours or less. A fish, well-fed late in the evening, may prowl for food towards dawn. Food taken in then is well digested by evening. Any daytime insect activity or availability can also trigger feeding responses, but there are usual feeding rhythms of early and late in the day throughout much of the season. As we've mentioned previously, trout see well during these periods of low level illumination and coincidentally feel more secure with regard to possible animal or bird predators. Dull overcast days or broken surfaces, distorted by current or wind, may also promote a greater than normal sense of security. In bright weather, when there is no insect activity to stimulate feeding responses or when temperatures are marginal, trout often retreat to cover beneath the mainstream currents, shadowy undercuts, boulders and the like. Here they may assimilate any food taken in, rest, minimize location indexing by various predators, and find a comfortable diffusion of light or shade.

Although there will always be unanswered and perhaps some unanswerable questions regarding trout behavior, all anglers can benefit from the reminder that we are dealing with a wary, well-adapted creature who is constantly alert to events around him. Any specifics of how well they can hear or see may be soon forgotten, but if we retain the overall impression of their capabilities it may help us slow down and be more careful in our approaches and presentations. Such considerations should prove bountiful over the long run.

# 13.

# FOOD FORMS

Trout food forms of potential importance to the angler are many and varied, including insects of both aquatic and terrestrial origins. Additionally, there are various baitfish, true bugs, and crustaceans which assume varying degrees of local or seasonal importance and require imitative efforts.

Within the rather elastic framework of aquatic insects, the most prominent are mayflies, stoneflies, caddis flies and various midges. Terrestrials may also be represented variously, but the primary imitative problems lie with grasshoppers, crickets, beetles, leafhoppers, inchworms and ants. True bugs may include water boatmen and backswimmers. Scuds and sow bugs are abundant in many fertile waters and may require suggestion. Baitfish comprise another wide range of opportunity with sculpin, dace, shiners, chubs, darters and others, including immature trout, showing up in the diet of large trout.

Since we are treading a fundamental path, discussion will be limited to rather general characteristics and habits. There is an abundance of excellent literature available for additional reference in keeping with an individual's developing attitudes and interests.

The mayflies spend most of their life underwater in immature stages of their growth cycle. By contrast, the winged adult stages are brief, typically one to three days. The life cycle consists of four states: egg, nymph, dun (or sub imago), and spinner (or imago). The latter three stages are of angling significance. Because there is no pupal stage, the life cycle is referred to as incomplete metamorphosis.

The usual life span of most species is about a year with a few of the smaller species being multibrooded within the framework of a single season. These non-typical species may have a life cycle of two to three months. Some of the largest, burrowing mayflies may require three years to complete their span.

Typically, the newly emerged nymph is almost microscopic. Most, but not all, are vegetarian and consume the diatoms and other microscopic plant organisms and occasionally chew at the tissues of higher plants. The numphs are enormous contributors to the life of fresh waters by changing plant life materials into animal tissue which can then serve as food for larger, predatory insects and higher forms such as the trout. Rather rapid nymph growth occurs. To accommodate this growth, the nymphs moult (twenty or even thirty times in some species). During the moult the nymph splits the restraining nymphal shuck at the thorax and head and struggles free. The nymph is typically pale, almost transparent, and defenseless until the chitin hardens in its new skin and normal coloration is regained. The period between moults is termed an instar.

Anglers tend to categorize mayfly nymphs into four approximate classifications depending on their nymphal habits. These categories recognize and differentiate the various specific adaptations to the aquatic communities in which they are found.

BURROWERS are usually found along the banks or in quiet stream stretches and pools as well as at the bottom of ponds and lakes. They are able to dig in the silt and fine gravel materials with their flattened, shelflike heads, large mandibular tusks, and flattened front legs. They feature long plumose gills, situated around upon their back so they are not injured when digging or burrowing. These gills are in almost constant motion to keep a current of water flowing. These nymphs are comparatively large and are usually less than two inches below the substratum surface, but they have been found to depths of several inches. On occasion they may be noted above the stream water line where they have dug into the wet banks. Their long, sweeping tails are visible as they project from their burrows.

CLINGERS are tenacious, fast-water dwellers, whose forms are greatly flattened. In most species the gills are platelike, overlapping to form a ventral suction disc. Heads are wide and eyes are located at the top lateral edge. Normally these have a single year life cycle.

SWIMMERS Depending on the species, they enjoy a range of water types. Body shapes are similar in that they are slender and cylindrical. The lentic or calm-water species have heavily fringed tails that provide propulsion in swimming. They climb about vegetation, darting in and out of shelter and occasionally swimming out into open water areas with excellent agility. Generally the calm-water species are small to medium in size. The lotic or running-water species are larger, although similar in habit and agility. When at rest they face upstream.

CRAWLERS may be found in various water types, but medium currents harbor the greatest numbers. As a group they are slightly depressed in shape or ovoid in cross-sectional shapes, thin tailed, and the gills are often reduced in number and are dorsal in position. They are poor swimmers and tend to walk about in the debris and bottom rubble, or sit, silt covered.

In all cases, when the elapsed time for the species involved has passed and suitable water temperatures are attained, the nymphs stop both feeding and growing. Wing pads or cases darken, becoming virtually black in some cases. Emergence to the air is accomplished in various ways: some migrate to the shallows or crawl out on rocks; some escape the restraining nymphal shuck at the stream bottom or within a few inches of the surface, emerging through the surface film as adult duns. Most species swim or struggle to the surface where, with the aid of the surface tension, they complete their transformation to the dun.

Mayfly emergence activity generally begins when water temperatures reach the upper forties to fifty degrees for a period of two to three days. This early season activity is typically in the afternoon when waters are at their warmest. The duration for any single species is normally from a few days to about ten days.

Fortunately nature is repeatable to the extent that the same species will emerge about the same time each year. Climatic variables may exert an influ-

*The mayfly dun exhibits an upright wing as opposed to the flattened wing of the adult stonefly or the tent wing shape of the caddis fly. Normally there is a second pair of wings of much reduced size—although this feature is lacking in a few species.*

ence by a factor of a few days one way or another. But, on the whole, the repeatability is surprising.

Colorations of the mayfly duns are various, ranging through mostly subdued shadings: early season's greyish/brownish values, various olive shadings, tan to medium brownish, creamy yellow to ginger and dark brownish, to almost black. Body lengths are obviously variable with different species and encompass a typical range from about one-eight of an inch to about one and one half inches.

On leaving the water, the dun seeks the comparative safety of streamside foliage. Not all enemies have been left behind when he escapes the trout. Those swooping and darting swallows, waxwings, and other birds capitalize on the abundant availability as well. Resting on the underside of leaves, the dun does not feed. Mouth parts have atrophied and are non-functional. In a span from almost immediate transformation to a period of about three days, but usually in one or two days, the skin slits along the back and the spinner (imago) emerges. The body color is more vibrant now, and the wings are often transparent or hyaline; tails are long and delicate, and the forelegs of the male become quite long. This second-winged stage is unique to the mayflies. Sexually mature now, many mating flights occur when air temperatures are in the sixty to seventy degree range. In the typical mating flight, the males appear over the water, rising and falling as a swarm. The females fly into the undulating swarm to secure mates. Mating occurs in flight and the female deposits the eggs to the water. Some are jettisoned above the surface, some species dip periodically to the surface, some lie prone to the surface, and the species of

*The mayfly spinner typically has a vibrantly colored body and transparent (hyaline) wings. The tails are lengthened. In the case of the males, the forelegs become quite long.*

As mayfly nymphs approach the time of transformation to winged adults, the wing pads typically darken and become almost black in some species.

At the time of the actual transformation, the thorax area splits and the adult mayfly dun struggles free of the restraining nymphal shuck.

*Baetis* crawl beneath the water surface to deposit their eggs.

The females then lie spent on the surface as do many males. However, some males survive another day or a few days before succumbing.

STONEFLIES: As you might imagine, the name is an implication of their preference for well-aerated, rocky, stream sections and in some cases, the wave-lapped, highly-oxygenated shallows of large lakes.

In a manner similar to the mayfly they have an incomplete metamorphis or life cycle consisting of egg, nymph, and adult. Depending on the species (some 400 occur in North America), the nymphs vary in size with average body lengths ranging from less than half an inch to about two inches. Underwater life spans range from a year to about three years. Colors vary with species. Some are almost uniform in coloration: cream, green, pale amber to brownish black and grayish black. Others exhibit a paling or lightening on their undersides and a few are quite striking in contrasting blacks and yellows. Their nymphal feeding habits are different according to the species, and the other includes vegetarians and carnivorous forms.

The stoneflies moult several times as they grow. When fully grown they migrate to favored rocks or to the shallows and climb out of the water. The thorax is split and the adult struggles free. Adults often rest for some time while the soft wings and body parts harden. Many emerge at night or very early in the day; occasionally some emerge during the day. Because emergences are often so slow, their favored nighttime and early day emergences are

*The stonefly nymphs are typically flattened in appearance, feature "double" wing pads, and prefer well-aerated stream sections.*

probably an adaptation to prevent predatory birds from truly devastating their ranks. Western anglers eagerly await the so-called salmon fly or willow fl hatches on large swift streams. These streams are ideally suited to the habit of the stonefly. Huge trout are willing to feed on these emergences.

Adult stoneflies are clumsy fliers. They almost appear to be walking or running through the air as they fly with their bodies held in an almost vertical position. The females of many species discharge the egg mass by dipping the

*The stone nymphs climb out of the water prior to transformation to the adult stage. The thorax and head area split and the emerging adult struggles free in a time-consuming process.*

*The stonefly adult features an elongated body. Its wings fold flat over the body when it is at rest.*

tip of the abdomen below the surface while in flight. This can trigger explosive rises from opportunistic trout. Except for mating flights, stoneflies are rarely over the water in great numbers. Still, there is a prolonged availability of one species or another throughout the season. Patterns tied to suggest the available stoneflies always offer potential success in appropriate waters.

Caddis are another insect of great importance to the angler. They have a complete metamorphosis consisting of egg, larva, pupa, and adult. Various species have adopted to life in virtually all water types. Some 800 species occur in North America. They are variable in length as larva, from the so-called micro caddis of one-eighth of an inch to lengths of some two inches. The larval forms are most interesting as many of them build protective cases about themselves, the cases cemented together by glandular secretions. Despite a possible rough exterior to the cases, the insides are quite smooth, allowing a freedom of movement. There are characteristic patterns within various species. Typical materials utilized are leaf fragments, sticks, bits of barks or twigs or other vegetation, sand grains, tiny stones, and even tiny shells. There is a seeming precision and uniformity. Most species repeatedly make the same type of case from the same materials.

As larva grows it adds to the cases. Often the larva lies with the head, thorax and legs outside the case and the body is mildly undulated to keep water circulating. Although some of the cases appear heavy and awkward, they are usually built by those living in fast waters where the weight is of anchoring value. Further, a bubble or two of air inside can provide buoyancy and make it relatively weightless. Some species do not build cases through the first few instars. Some remain free living throughout their larval life span. These build a silken net or tube so fastened to stones that the current washes through it. The larva lying in a silken or stonewalled retreat nearby can feed on the trapped food forms. Some construct partial cases, faced with the silken nets behind which the larval forms remain to feed on tiny organisms trapped in the netting. All these larva forms are of value to trout food and many imitations exist. Most imitations suggest the round-bodied, wormlike larva alone; some few attempt to suggest the cased larva, for trout consume larva and case when given the opportunity. They eventually pass the bits of bark and twigs or whatever, while their digestive processes utilize the larva.

The pupal stage follows the larval stage. Often this is a ten-day and two-week period. Adult characteristics begin to appear as the transformation takes place. The retreat makers construct an elliptical cocoon in which they pupate. Case makers pupate within their own case. They may cement the case down. It may have a silken screen spun across the opening, or a protective pebble may block the opening. The pupa typically remain active within the case, undulating the body to provide water motion.

When the proper elapsed time has been achieved, the pupa cuts out of the restraining case and swims or struggles to the surface. At the surface the pupa husk ruptures and the adult emerges. Some caddis complete this change on the bottom and swim to the surface and out of the water. Some slow-water species

86

crawl to the shallows and emerge like stone flies.

Caddis emergences are productive times for the angler. Trout must actively chase moving species. Tell-tale rolling and splashing may indicate activity. Surface disturbances are possible during pupal activity as the trout roll and slash near the surface. Unless the surface rise form is accompanied by a bubble

*Many caddis larvae inhabit protective cases that are striking and distinctive by species. At left is a larva form in a case of vegetative fragments. At right a stone or pebble protective case. At front right is a caddis larva that has been removed from its case.*

*The caddis fly adult has a distinctive "tent wing" appearance making it easily distinguishable from the flat wing stoneflies or the upright wing mayfly forms.*

or bubbles, the pupal suggestions are apt to be most appropriate. Adult caddis are obviously fine fare for the trout as well. During egg laying activity there may be fine trout activity. Some species oviposit over the water, some dip the eggs into the stream itself, some species go beneath the surface to oviposit directly on the bottom. All activities lend themselves to succesful imitation. Various caddis may be expected to be available on a season long basis.

The midges of the order *Diptera* encompass every aquatic community. Yet the greatest angling potential may well lie in lush, weedy areas, slower stream sections, and ponds and lakes. The high altitude ponds at or above timberline are other general locations where midge imitations may be essential to success. Many larger aquatic forms are not universally represented in the high country, yet some midge forms are almost always available and assume a very significant importance in spite of their relative size.

There is a complete metamorphosis of egg, larva, pupa and adult. The latter three stages are worthy of imitation. Despite their relative size, typically one-eighth to half an inch, the virtual season-long availability of the differing forms plus their vast numerical abundance and relative ease of capture requires imitations at one time or another.

The round-bodied larva come in different colors. Commonly they are red, yellowish, almost translucent white, greenish, grey or brownish black. For practical reasons involving their small size and ease of strike detection, the larva imitations are best presented gently to visibly feeding fish. It is possible to fish them deeply with slow retrieves, but on the whole you'll be more concerned with near surface activity.

Many species spend the day deep and rise toward the surface with approaching evening. In those magic twilight moments the trout may be apparently rising but not moving to your tiny dries. They may pluck at leader knots and you'll see them roll and flash. Even backs or tails will disturb the surface. Most likely larval or pupal imitations are required when the dries drift unmolested by the abundant and active trout. After the larva transforms to the pupal stage, there is ample evidence of the ultimate adult. Differing from the roundish, wormlike larva, the pupa shows definite hairy appendages at the head and tail, folded (but visible on close inspection) wings, as well as obvious thorax enlargement. These drifting pupa are taken avidly. During the transformation from pupa to adult there is trout activity. The transformation is time consuming and they are exteemely vulnerable. Adults typically are mosquitolike in appearance and may sit quietly on the water for some time before taking flight. Again, a period of vulnerability.

Start with tiny dries during this action. If they aren't effective, the pupal or larval imitations should be tried. Get a sample of the insect to determine developmental stage, form, and color. This is usually possible. There may also be a hint available in inspection of the rise-form type. If you've ever tried to pick an insect from water by letting it wash into your hand, you've found it impossible. The surface tension diverts the insect around your hand. The trout has a similar problem, but also has a built-in solution. He flares his gills, and the insect, air, and water are taken in. Then the air is expelled through the gills, leaving a bubble or bubbles in the wake of the rise form. If bubbles exist in the rise form, it is likely the insect was taken in or on the surface. An appropriate imitation may be used. Without the bubble evidence, more than likely a pupa or larva imitation should be fished just beneath the surface. This bubble evidence has other applications. Was the trout slashing to the caddis pupa barely beneath the surface or to the emerged adult, the barely subsurface mayfly nymph or the adult? Such clues or signals sometimes help us sort out the probabilities, guiding us to appropriate fly type selection.

Another relative deserves at least passing mention: the crane fly. The larva are wormlike, typically from half an inch to about two inches, with colorations varying from a whitish shading through pale orange tones to various brownish shadings. The larva will often be grubbed off the bottom. Imitiations fished on a deep, dead, drift can be effective. Most (not all) pupate out of water and are not important to the angler. Adults may be suggested by various, high-riding, sparse types, such as spiders, skaters, and variants, although there are a few specific patterns tied for a more precise imitation of the adult's gangly, spraddle-legged posture.

Let's glance at a few other important insects. From the insect order *Odonata* there are dragon flies and damselflies. Generally the nymphal imitations are more successful than the adult imitations, although some effective adult imitations do exist. Nymphal forms of these two insects are visibly distinguishable. The damselflies are slender and minnowlike with a body terminating in three flat gills. Dragonflies are husky, almost muscular in appearance. Although modes of locomotion differ, both are capable of active movement. They are predatory forms ranging about the bottom amidst the weed beds, searching for their food forms. Sunken suggestions fished in a stuttering pause and pull motion can be very effective. Towards emergence time they crawl from the water and ascend reeds and plant stems. Their empty husks may be seen in a manner similar to the stone flies, and their discarded nymphal shucks can be found on stream rocks. Emergence takes place early in the day and is also time consuming. The adults are at first soft bodied with a shriveled abdomen and crumpled wings. Before they can take off, they must extend their abdomen and expand and dry their wings. Once more, this early emergence probably takes place to avoid predatory birds which would be active at later hours. Nymphal colors are usually in the olive to greenish brown values. At times windy days and egg laying activities provide good activity for the adult suggestions, but the nymph patterns generally do better.

The hellgrammite and the allied alderflies and fishflies may be of seasonal or local importance. The hellgrammite is a highly regarded bass bait which is also effective on large trout. It is the larva of the huge dobsonfly. As larva they are secretive and have a long, three-year life cycle. Consequently they are available to fish in a range of sizes up to three inch monsters. Imitations of one and one quarter inch to two inches are most productive. They handle well and move fish nicely. The larva have a flattened, busy-looking appearance with tufted gills along the sides. The brownish black imitations should be fished in the swift sections where the natural larvae are abundant.

The alderflies have a basic larval shape similar to the hellgrammite but are considerably smaller: about one inch or a bit less. The larva are brownish and thick skinned with a single-fringed tail gill. Adults are caddislike in appearance and are often active in bright spring sunlight. The aquatic habitat includes ponds, lakes and streams. The alderfly pattern is an effective imitiation of the smokey to dark-winged flies.

In the fishfly there is again a superficial resemblance to the larger hellgram mite, yet the fringed gills are lacking, The fishfly lateral gills are slender. Also there are no strong mandibles as on the hellgrammite. Fishflies are more widely distributed in various water types. A typical larval imitation of about one inch is effective in dark brownish to brownish black values.

The small crustacea that assume significant value in weedy streams and ponds are the scuds and sow bugs. Often they are called freshwater shrimp by anglers. The scuds are from the order *Amphipoda*. You may also hear them referred to as side swimmers. Shrimplike in appearance, they are flattened sideways or laterally compressed. These omnivorous scavengers feed on plant and animal debris. In turn they are consumed by trout in large numbers. They lie close to the bottom or among submerged weed growths in ponds and slow flowing streams, and are especially abundant in rich alkaline waters. The sizes vary from $^3/_8$ to almost an inch. The colors are typically grayish, yellowish gray, tan to light brown, and olive. They move on their sides by flexing and extending their entire body and frequently rolling on their sides or back. The bodies are held out straight while swimming.

The sow bugs are from the order *Isopoda* and are often abundant in rich alkaline waters amidst watercress and weed where they are omnivorous scav engers. They are seldom in open water. Most species prefer shallow waters. Average sizes may be from about a quarter of an inch to a bit over half an inch. Most are uniformly gray, or almost black. A few are brownish, reddish, or yellowish. They have a flattened appearance and feature fourteen legs. Imita tions of these dead bugs drifted by the weed bed edges are effective.

Crayfish are from the order *Decapoda*. They too may be quite appealing to large trout, although not too many imitations are generally available. Although they can reach large sizes, your imitations are best in the smaller sizes for reasons of reasonable suggestion, handling ease, and a fish preference for the smaller, more manageable sizes. Imitations can be moved over those rocky runs where the naturals preside. Very early in the day and very late, even into darkness, are apt to be the most productive times. Many of the larger trout in late spring have eaten crayfish. These are a vastly overlooked possibility for big trout.

The bugs of aquatic representation are from the order *Hemiptera*. The water boatman or corixa bug are common to shallow waters of ponds, lakes and streams. Many species are dark grayish and often mottled with dark brownish black and may be faintly cross lined with yellow. Their long hind legs are flattened for swimming and extend out, like the backswimmers, and can propel the bug along with strong oarlike strokes. They are very buoyant. When submerged they must hold onto plants or weeds or other objects to remain submerged. They dive with great ease and agility, and air taken in at the surface usually surrounds them in a silvery envelope. A typical imitation may be about a quarter inch in overall body length.

The backswimmers have a boat-shaped or keeled back and paddlelike legs

The hind legs are longer than the middle and front legs. They hold an air supply on the underside of their bodies and beneath the wings, and come to the surface periodically to rest and replenish their air supply by sticking the tip of their abdomens above the surface. They can and will bite sharply. When diving or beneath the surface they exhibit a silvery envelope of air bubbles and are capable of moving with excellent agility. Of the various species, the most common is about half an inch long with a dark brownish olive body and light and dark mottling of the wing cases.

The leeches of the class *Hirudinea* are another, occasionally important, food form. They are usually dorsoventrally flattened, sometimes brightly colored, and patterned in green and black. Some species swim well, others swim poorly. In the last few years commercial "snakelike" patterns have become available and have proven quite effective on large trout.

The land dwelling terrestrial insects are not aquatic but leap, tumble, or are blown to the water with some regularity and become important food forms. The more important imitative problems usually center around grasshoppers, crickets, beetles, leafhoppers, inchworms and ants (both winged and without wings). Each of these forms exhibit a distinctive shape or silhouette that can be suggested by widely available commercial patterns.

The baitfish constitute another realm of opportunity and imitative potential. There are various shiners, chubs, darters, dace, sculpin and others, including imitations of small trout that can work well. These serve as prototypes for a host of streamer-bucktail patterns. Have some of those forms available in the waters you fish, and back this up with a couple of bright, attractor patterns for those times when the water is off color or when you've run out of better ideas.

*Lefty Kreh fishing on the Savage River in western Maryland's mountains.*

# 14.

# READING WATER

## Streams

Learning to read water is an acquired skill. Experience is the best teacher. Admittedly this takes time, but the novice may be able to hasten the process by enlisting the aid of an experienced angler. Invariably such experienced hands are more than willing to assist and explain why trout station themselves at definite stream locations. In your own early angling experiences think about why the trout rising are rising where they are, what combination of currents and nearby cover exists, where the emerging insects are drifting, and what are the feeding lies of the trout. All these bits and pieces of information eventually sort themselves·out and an instinct for rapid and accurate appraisal develops.

To assist in this learning process we can cover some of the fundamental considerations affecting their location. The primary need of the trout is security: protection or concealment from potential predators. They also seek protection from very strong mainstream currents which would rapidly tire them. They do, however, like to have a current flow nearby for food forms on the assorted drift which the current brings. Another obvious requirement is suitable water temperature. In critically warm situations they seek out spring holes, cold water seepages, and areas of the stream with increased oxygen contents or cooler temperatures. For our introductory purposes we can assume water temperatures to be suitable and simply examine some typical situations.

Trout are both territorial and dominant. Invariably the better fish select and maintain the best feeding and sheltering lies. We should also note that water velocity is not constant from top to bottom. This becomes apparent when standing in a waist deep flow of water. The surface flow tugs at our waist, at our upper thighs we feel a faster current force being exerted, while at our booted feet a much reduced velocity is noticed. The current similarly slows near large obstructions and along stream banks, for friction causes a lateral slow-down. The water close to the bank runs slower than the main current just a short distance away.

These considerations have important bearings on trout locations. For instance, in moderately deep runs the fish show an unequal distribution from top to bottom. Beneath the strong current of the main run the bottom is apt to be rocks, boulders, and gravel. There is already a quiet cushion of water close to the bottom and the presence of such rocks further deflects and cushions the flow. The depth of water is ideal concealment and provides the diffusion of light or shade which is more comfortable to the lidless eye of the trout. Many bottom-dwelling food forms exist here, and other stream-drifted insects and food forms which are washed deep may be easily snapped up. These deep runs deserve investigative probings with your flies or lures. If an emergence of insects is taking place, the trout may be holding high, a few inches from the surface, with their attention on the drifting flies. If the main current is too forceful for a comfortable position maintenance, they move to the side of the main currents or drop back in the run to a point where velocities are reduced and they may hold with relative ease.

The undercut banks are excellent locations. There is overhead cover and a cushioning zone of quiet water with easy access to a primary, food-supplying current.

Although some food develops in virtually all water types, the stream riffle areas are most important in this respect. If they are very shallow the fish may only move in when foraging actively or during an emergence of insects. The diminished light values of predawn and evening may bring foraging fish into these areas. If, by chance, the riffle is a couple of feet deep, it could be considered a trout holding possibility at any time and fished through thorough-ly.

The riffles typically shelve or drop into a pool. Toward the head of the pool is the deeper water. With any kind of appropriate bottom structure, trout may be expected to hold here in comfort. These fish have first opportunity at food drifting into the pool. When a hatch is in progress they simply move up towards the surface to feed. If the main current tongue is too swift, they again migrate to the current edges or drop back in the pool to a point where the current force is diminished and they can comfortably hold and feed. It's also possible that some fish will move directly up into the riffle area ahead of the pool. At the tail of the pool the water shallows and may, if cover is available, provide another fine lie. Many times appropriate tail cover is lacking and fish move back into these tailing shallows only when in a definite feeding posture.

The long flat stretches of shallow, slow-moving water can be very deceptive. They deserve a look before you pass premature judgment and hurry on. There is a particular stretch of a nearby river that is overlooked on one side by a high bank. From it the stretch appears absolutely barren. Mainstream bottom cover

94

is virtually nonexistent and every pebble and grain of sand seems visible. Yet every summer evening there are quiet rise forms here and there, especially close to the opposite shore. Wading over and walking slowly along that far bank reveals a few of the secrets. There is an occasional deeper depression in the stream bed, perhaps scoured by a current deflection in the high water of spring. There are occasional hollowed out root structures among the streamside willows. Another depression exists in the stream bottom behind the fallen tree. Each, by itself, seems insignificant, but they total up to a dozen or more individual lies that contain a trout or two. It's tough water to "just fish," but during any emergence activity the trout become vulnerable to careful stalking and deliberate presentations. Easily overlooked, this is proof that trout can seemingly disappear into the strangest places.

The pocket water stretches are quickly flowing currents, diverted and broken by boulders and large rocks. The obstructions provide any number of quiet water cushions and hiding places. Pocket water also harbors excellent insect populations. During periods of warm water there are increased oxygen levels here as compared to other water types. This is an obvious attraction for the comfort-seeking trout. Waterfall pools may also prove productive, especially when the pool bottom is broken and diverse with rocks or sunken logs.

Some streams have a steep gradient, which puts a premium on short, quick and accurate casting. Many anglers bypass the bubbly waters formed as the currents flow smooth and slick over the rocks and drop down into what might be called miniature waterfalls. But that bubbly water is often productive. The water flow energy is actually dissipated for a brief moment before it gathers and flows on. Insects washed into these areas may be submerged and swirled about helplessly before being pushed on downstream. I've often found trout willing to take large nymphs or wets plopped into these areas when other water types were non-productive.

Some stream banks also provide hiding and feeding areas, and not all of these are obvious. Some are insignificant in initial appearance. There is a good example nearby in the midst of a heavily fished section of stream. Few bother with this particular site. Standing below it and looking upstream we see the left bank shelving very gradually off into the stream, providing no semblance of cover or concealment. The right hand bank is low and inconspicuous but it is tree lined and the small current that comes through here is diverted toward that right side bank. The browns that take up residence here find shelter in washed out root structures along that right hand bank. During emergence activity they move out mere inches. This is a consistent producer to those in the know. Activity is always quiet, always tight by the bank, and the average angler wanders by with a cursory glance that fails to reveal the real value of this run. Similar situations exist on all trout waters.

Meadow stream banks offer a modified, but essentially parallel situation with their numerous undercuts and overhanging grasses. The bank-feeding fish with their quiet, unhurried rise forms are often the largest fish that surface-feed on these streams. On spring creeks and those weedy multi-channeled streams, the bank edges must also be watched carefully. Also there are excellent insect and crustacean populations in the abundant watercress and islands of *elodea* of these stream types. These weeds form obstructions that divert the flow and

*Western meadow streams may provide exceptional angling. Watch the stream banks for quiet rise forms which may mask large trout.*

*With numerous rocks and obstructions to deflect main current flows and provide cushions of quiet water for the trout, this section of a western river offers excellent angling potential.*

create channels in the same manner that fallen trees and rocks might do on another water type. These channels should be probed by the thorough angler.

By reading a stream you're trying to locate those areas where security for the trout is available with a potential feeding area nearby: those areas where fast and slow waters merge; those slow-water "islands" in the midst of faster flows; sunken logs lying parallel to the current flow; eddying currents supporting trapped insect forms; currents rejoining below islands that have split and diverted the main flow; edges where shallow water falls abruptly off to deeper areas; above, below and beside large in-stream rocks and other singular obstructions. These and more are all typical. As we've said previously, when you see activity, try to analyze why it is taking place and where it is taking place. Trout activity is not random. The more bits and pieces of information you file away, the quicker and more accurate your future stream reading appraisals will be.

# Ponds and Lakes

Ponds and lakes are inherently more difficult to analyze. The moving water of a stream always provides clues that eventually become familiar and meaningful. The lake surface is simply there, almost defying you to probe for its secrets. Just as there are various stream types, there are different lake and pond types. A backwoods pond at 2500 feet in the Adirondacks is a different situation than a pond tucked away at 10,000 feet on a Colorado mountain. Still, there are possibilities in each, not the least of which is fine angling for large fish.

Cherished by many is the discovery of a newly formed beaver pond. Intimate and newly enriched, rapid trout growth occurs. Eventually the waters become much too acidic and warm, causing the trout population to rapidly decline. But, these ponds at their prime offer excellent potential. Their dark waters are best probed with wet flies, nymphs, or midget streamers, unless definite surface activity is taking place. Wading the small beaver ponds with their soft muck and debris is distrubing, difficult, and potentially dangerous. Crouching and creeping along the stick jam platform is usually possible. The old mainstream channel is apt to be productive when the fish are down during bright sunlight days. Any cruising activity near shore or around still, standing trees will be self-evident when it occurs. A small inflatable boat or float tube may be advantageous on some waters.

In New England the beaver pond specialists are very secretive, realizing that such waters have a short productive cycle. One individual, in addition to his own locating efforts, is continually probing the local trappers, hunters, hikers, anglers, and wardens to learn of new sites from year to year. Any possibilities are carefully marked on a topo map for further investigation.

Another overlooked resource is by any swampy area that is either the headwater area of a stream or a portion of the lake itself. A small inflatable boat or float tube is often required, but these areas are sometimes deep, clear, spring fed and almost undisturbed.

In general the food generating areas of lakes are shallow, to the depths of sunlight penetration. Deep waters located near such shallows provide an escape route for wary trout. Whenever there are shallows which suddenly fall away to the depths, they are potentially excellent feeding sites, especially early and late in the day. Out on the lake proper near any island there is often a bouldery bottom for a short distance until another abrupt drop-off occurs. Shoals or reefs that swell up close to the surface are also potential feeding areas.

Spring hole locations are excellent during periods of hot weather and are apt to draw concentrations of trout seeking relief from the excessively warm surrounding waters. Tom Sobolewski, who operates Clark's Tackle in Lake Placid, advised Tony Atwill and I that he often swims his favorite Adirondack ponds to find these spring hole locations. Several hot hours later as Tony and I backpacked into a reasonably offbeat area of the western Adirondacks, the words of Tom Sobolewski seemed to make a lot of sense. However, when we stood at the shoreline of our destination and noticed several leeches, apparently just waiting for us, we decided to abandon any swimming in favor of our inflatable boats. Several times spring holes will be marked by a single "push pole." Someone has previously pinpointed the location and marked it by shoving a long branch into the bottom. When these seem to appear at random in odd locations they are worth checking out on remote waters. *New York Times* outdoor columnist Nelson Bryant is an experienced outdoorsman with a special affinity for remote ponds. He thoroughly believes in deeply sunken flies worked around spring hole locations during midsummer heat on his favored northeastern ponds. On a day hike into the Green Mountain National Forest area, Nelson was actively moving about the pond in his inflatable boat, trying to locate those elusive drop-offs and spring holes. Using a rock as an anchor and a probe he began searching according to a theory he attributed to Thoreau: ". . . the deepest part of the pond is often where imaginary lines, connecting its longest and widest parts, intersect."

Additionally, the inlets and outlets of lakes are always worth investigation as well as any thoroughfares between a series of ponds or lakes.

In weedy waters the channels between the emergent growth should be probed thoroughly. These waters are rich in insect and crustacean life forms and are often superb for large trout. On weedy waters the dragonfly and damselfly nymphs often move toward emergent weed growths early in the predawn. Husky trout follow suit. Sunken imitations, fished in a stuttering pause and pull manner may be productive. It is certainly a good idea to watch the surface in the evening. Just as on the streams, the pond-dwelling trout often forage actively early and late in the day. At times help may be available in the form of a distinctive shoreline. For example, a gradually sloping shoreline usually continues to fall away underwater. A steep shoreline falling sharply to the lake probably continues the same way underwater. There may be several

*Float tubes or belly boats can be a valuable addition for the angler/backpacker, permitting water coverage that would otherwise be impossible.*

feet of water close to shore with a bouldery, rock strewn bottom that offers food and cover. Check to see if there is any regional or local fishing literature showing pond or stream drop-offs.

Lake fish also cruise for food. If they are rising, the experienced angler will watch the direction of the rises and then lead the fish by casting well ahead of their travel direction. Watch too, for feeding lanes on breezy days when the surface drift is being blown toward windward shores. Sometimes there will be slicks of calmer water with trout cruising the area for trapped insect forms.

If the winds come up strong they may cause a good feeding period along the windward shore. Early in the windy period the best activity is at or near the surface. If the winds continue, fish tend to switch and work deeper as the continuing wave action ultimately sets up a return current flow deep beneath the surface influence.

The ponds that lie at high altitudes are a variation of the overall problem. There is apt to be a less diverse aquatic community. Generally the most important high country food forms are scuds, midges, mayflies, caddis flies, and terrestrials, although their relative importance varies from one body of water to another. Sometimes there is one or two minnow species available even though the so-called trash fish are virtually non-existent at these altitudes. These high country waters may be the ultimate for the backpacking angler, lying in regions of majestic beauty and solitude. The weather is variable to say the least, the seasons are short, and winterkill of fish may be a problem in some shallow waters. But, if you are at the right place at the right time, there is nothing quite like it. High country specialists utilize inlets and outlets the same way that we would check these areas at lower altitudes. Look for various natural drainage areas as well. These are sites where snow melt, springs, or rain runoffs have gone into the pond. Fish sometimes gather at these sites despite the original water source possibly having dried up. Very early and late in the day, the best location is often a shelf that may extend out into the lake for a short distance, then abruptly drops off to much deeper water. If you have a float tube or inflatable boat along, cast from the deep open water back towards this shelf, working the fly in the direction of the deep water. If there is no tube or boat, try casts made parallel to this shelf (unless there is specific, visible activity to zero in on).

Any points of land that extend into the pond are also worth looking into. Cruising trout have to go around these points and may come within easy reach of the bank-bound angler.

Ponds and lakes may be considerably different than the flowing waters of the streams but, in time, they too will reveal their secrets to your advantage.

# 15.
# INTRODUCTION TO METHODS

The freedom of travel associated with backpacking permits access to a variety of water types and sizes. Thus an overview of a typical stream course should help the novice angler anticipate angling requirements. Most streams are zonally divisible. Their characteristics change greatly from the headwater areas to the ultimate destination where the stream joins a larger river system, lake, or ocean. Some of the differences are physical size, width, depth, flow volume, water types, gradient, and temperature ranges. These differences have some bearing on typical angling approaches, the food forms available to the trout, and the species of trout in numerical dominance.

In hilly or mountainous country the upper reaches are usually small, intimate, well aerated, often tree canopied and shady with cooler average temperatures being maintained through the midsummer heat. Because of the intimate nature of the small stream, there is a close association with shore life in that some terrestrials such as ants, beetles, and crickets fall or tumble to the water regularly to supplement the aquatic insect availability. Those streams with headwaters in meadowy areas also contribute quantities of grasshoppers seasonally. The intimate, generally shallower waters imply easier animal and diving bird predator access. The dominant trout populations tend to be those which do best in non-competetive situations or those with a preference for cooler average water temperatures (i.e. western cutthroat and eastern brook trout). Available aquatic insect forms are less varied and less abundant than in lower stream sections. The midges, cased and net spinning caddis, small mayfly nymphs, some stoneflies in the quicker runs, and perhaps a minnow species or two usually are the dominant food forms.

If there are occasional deeper holes, runs or undercuts, these tend to be the prime locations for the occasional mini-stream native trophy. There may be seasonal headwater penetration or migration from other species as spring-spawning rainbows or fall-spawning browns move up. Also, if lower stream stretches become unsuitably warm in midsummer dry spells, there may be some migration of larger mainstream fish working up these cooler tributaries and headwater areas. In the event there is adequate cover and food, a few of these larger fish may take up permanent residence. The vast majority simply drop back down to the larger water areas as it becomes appropriate to do so. Still, I've seen many an outsize trout in streams that could be jumped across in many places.

*A fine Cutthroat from a small spring creek near Jackson Hole, Wyoming.*

These intimate little waters have an intrigue all their own. Pleasant and productive, they are the stream types most commonly associated with back-pack angling. There is less stream pressure, summer temperatures are cooler, and the trout are less selective as natural food availability is more restricted. Certainly most of the trout run to the small sizes, but there are those occasional large fish bonuses. Besides, the backpacking angler's equipment needs are minimal. Usually wading is neither required nor is it recommended. A careful shorebound approach supplemented by occasional judicious rock hopping or just plain wet wading will do the trick. Exercise care in stream approaches, utilizing natural cover whenever possible and keep clothing on the drab, incon-spicuous side. Work progressively but fairly rapidly for best results. The light-weight spin fisherman will find tiny spinners productive with lightweight plugs, jigs and spoons also appropriate for the occasional deep holes, runs, or dark undercuts. The fly rodder can get by with just a floating line in most such waters. If flies need to be worked deep, the addition of a split shot or twist-on lead about eighteen inches above the fly is usually adequate. The available food forms imply that small dries, wets, nymphs, a couple of terrestrials, and a midget streamer or bucktail are appropriate.

*Brushy, snaggy streams are common in many areas and can provide excellent fishing. Here, Dick Pobst works close to the cover.*

By midsummer on those mountain streams with a steep gradient, some of the better fish lurk by and beneath the bubbly areas formed as the water flows over the rocks and drops into the heads of pools. Since trout are opportunistic, large high floating patterns are surprisingly effective. These big dries are durable, visible, and tempting. Some of the types well suited to this prospecting are the Wulff patterns, the Humpy, the Irresistible, and any of the Bivisibles. Try #10's, even on small streams. If a large fish swirls and misses, reference the spot for a bit later. Chances are he'll move to the fly again. This is usually upstream work, except when unusual stream configurations call for approaching from above and drifting a fly down into the best cover.

Further downstream the gradient lessens and the stream begins to broaden. These midreaches are generally the peak trout fishing sections of the entire stream. Water types may be diverse with larger pools, runs, riffles, and pocket water alternately available. Temperatures are more moderate than in the headwater areas and the aquatic communities show much greater diversification as appropriate habitat and food is available to them in greater abundance.

The conventional stream-bred insects as well as various crustaceans and an expanded baitfish community may all be on hand and require simulation. Typically, browns and rainbows dominate these middle reaches. Angling methods are more diverse and there are periods of selective feeding. In the heat of summer the most appropriate times to fish are early and late in the day unless specific insect activity is taking place which tempts the trout to active feeding.

The lower stream sections often become marginal trout waters as streams flatten out, coursing the valley floor. They are typically wider, deeper, much warmer, and offer less diversity of water type. As temperatures become more suitable to other species such as bass, pike, panfish, etc., these fish begin to dominate. Trout are few, but often very large. Big browns seem especially adept at locating the right combination of depth, cover, or cooling temperature influence from spring seepages or incoming tributaries. They wax fat on the abundance of forage fish and other food forms. Fishing is slow and, to an extent, specialized. Generally dry fly moments are rare, but the prospecting and persistent angler adept at handling deeply sunken nymphs, wets, and streamers may hook a real trophy brown.

Thus, the course of a single stream will ultimately demand a variety of techniques and methods. The beginning angler is advised to maintain an open mind toward these requirements and utilize whatever method is suitable to the water and the activity. Many fly fishermen develop a strong preference for a particular method and use it to the exclusing of more appropriate methods. Obviously any individual preference is defensible from a standpoint of enjoyment, but it also limits fish-taking potential. I feel that this limits the total enjoyment available from the sport. Each method (dry, wet, nymph, terrestrial or streamer) has much to offer. Each is complex enough so that complete books can, have been, and will continue to be written about the subtle nuances of each. The novice angler is advised to follow up our introductory theme by studying more complete references.

The wet fly is a versatile approach which has been neglected in recent years as increased emphasis has been placed on nymph pattern and method development. The wet approach is usually considered to be broadly suggestive of aquatic activity, whereas the nymph implies greater specificity of imitation. Frequently the distinctions are blurred and there is some obvious overlapping of the two methods. Normally trout are specific and selective in their feeding when there is an adequate availability of a food form to warrant such exclusivity; the remainder of the time their activity is non-specific and opportunistic. Therefore, the impressionistic wet fly is frequently a sound starting point with which to search the water. Since it is suggestively lifelike there is a great deal of latitude hidden in the method: casts can be angled toward any compass point, the stream can be worked in up or down directions; the flies may dead drift or be animated variously; the working of all different water levels from the surface film down through middepths and gravel scratching levels is possible. The use of more than one fly on a single leader offers possible variations in the drifting depths of the flies as well as contrast in pattern, size, and tonal value.

Searching the water should be done in a thoroughly progressive manner with casting cycles hitting nearby water first then gradually radiating out to cover medium distances and finally the longer fishing arcs.

On a seasonal basis, the early mayflies tend to do quite a bit of drifting and spasmodic struggling to escape the nymphal shuck. The cast directed somewhat up and across stream and then permitted to alternately dead drift and twitch gently is often effective.

Another staple approach is the natural or dead drift. Of the various ways to achieve this, one of the best is to direct the cast well upstream and across with enough slack to permit the start of a free drift. As the slack is taken up by the current the line is mended to compensate and restore the free drifting motion of the artifical. Mending is simply throwing a loop of line up or downstream, whichever will permit the continuation of the drift. As the fly passes across stream from you and continues downstream, it is continually mended as required. This creates the illusion of the detached helpless insect form at the mercy of the current, assures a drift in harmony with existing current flows, and the fly is apt to remain sideways to that flow (the most visible position to the upstream facing trout). Across and downstream from you the fly will begin to elevate and move slightly towards your side of the stream on the tightening line. Many strikes occur here as the illusion is that of an insect suddenly coming to life and heading for the surface and airborne safety. If no strikes occur, the line continues to swing, coming to rest directly downstream from your position. It should not be immediately retrieved as it can become subject to various possibilities. Hold it steady, animate it by slowly raising and lowering the rod, raise the rod slowly towards the vertical and then lower it and shake out additional slack. Or, if there is deep cover along your side, lower the rod tip to the stream bed and retrieve the fly deep and close to the open side of the cover. Browns especially like overhead cover and a fly must work very deep to be seen.

At times a cross-stream swim is excellent. Take a position opposite or a bit above the suspected lie of the fish and drop the fly a few feet upstream and a bit beyond the lie of the fish. When the fly touches the surface allow it to dead drift across the hoped for taking lie or, more commonly, elevate the rod to keep as much line as possible off the water and flutter the fly back across the stream. This is especially telling in a two-fly set up with the twitching flies activiated by rod tip or line-hand manipulations. The two-fly approach is also good on cross and downstream presentations. About the easiest method of rigging up is to simply extend the heavier material end used when connecting leader sections in a barrel knot.

Another quick way to add a dropper to a knotted leader is to take a short section of separate monofilament and form a loop in one end. Then, loop it around the main body of the leader above a leader knot. It will hold in place against the leader knot. Keep the dropper strands on the short side, say four to six inches. If flies of different sizes are being used in a two-fly setup the larger of the two normally goes on the end of the leader and the smaller one on the dropper strand. The starting point is contrast in size, pattern, and color. Broken pocket water usually fishes well to the two-fly approach. Work a short line and allow the flies to drift and drag naturally in and out of quiet waters below and beside the stream obstructions. When natural drifts fail to produce, work cross-stream casts with the rod elevated and strip the flies. The dropper should alternately skim the surface, become elevated and drag below the surface.

Another appropriate time for a pair of wets is after a midsummer rain with the stream rising and becoming discolored. Nymphs and streamers also produce well at this time, but the down and across approach of a pair of wets usually works.

On small streams, and when fish are working near the top on larger waters, the floating line is adequate. For greater depths the sinktip or true sinking line may be more appropriate.

The basic nymphing methods encompass all the standard wet fly approaches and add a few singular opportunities. A very effective fast-water, short-line deeply sunken method involves a well-greased floating line (and it's usually preferable to grease the upper two feet or so of the leader butt), twist-on leads and a weighted nymph. The leader should be long, about twelve or more feet. Although various casting angles are possible, the usual approach is upstream and somewhat across. After the cast is made, the line is brought to the rod-

*Mending line is required to restore or maintain a natural drift in all fly rodding methods. With the rod in front, roll or flip the rod up or down stream, whichever is required. Mending corrections vary from short and subtle tip motions to vigorous full arm mends depending on conditions.*

holding hand. All retrieves are done behind this hand. As this is a dead drift method, there should be no line drag. Usually it is best to strip the line and let it drop rather than to try coiling it in the line hand. Any belly formed by varying current speeds must be removed, so mending compensations are required. As the fly drifts back downstream, the rod is elevated and the line-leader junction is above the surface. Rivet your attention on this, as the deeply sunken takes are short and subtle. If no strikes have occurred, permit the fly to continue downstream. Sometimes a fish will hit as the line tightens downstream and the fly responds by moving up off the bottom.

In very heavy, turbulent water a variation with a heavy sinking line, short leader and, a weighted stonefly numph works well. A short upstream cast is made, slack is recovered as needed, and once again as the fly passes your position the rod is well-elevated, then gradually lowered as the fly works on its downstream course. If anything, a slight influence on the fly helps; that is, the rod can lead the line as it comes downstream so the fish take solidly. Downstream and across a snappy, tip-jerking motion can bring the fly up towards the

*Charles Loughridge working a deeply sunken nymph on a Colorado stream.*

surface. Large stoneflies can scramble when they're disturbed, and strikes are hard.

Casts can also be directed across and downstream in choppy, boulder-studded water with a large nymph and the line type dictated by the depth of the water: a floater for near surface work, a sinktip or sinking line for deeper work.

Another effective time for nymphs is prior to and during an emergence of insects. There are dry fly parallels as a floating line and a single nymph usually work best. The fish are holding high in the water, visible to the angler, and can be approached with an up-and-cross stream cast. The line and perhaps the upper part of the leader should be well-greased. If the fish is easily visible, he should give an indication of the take. Or, watch closely where the leader penetrates the surface film and react to any sudden deviation from its normal drift. Should it stop, draw under the surface, or suddenly dart forward, it's a signal to strike quickly. Upstream dead drift methods when you're just covering the water, placing the nymph in likely feeding sites, or working with a longer line in difficult lighting conditions can be assisted by a strike detector of some kind. The innovative angler, Dave Whitlock, has popularized one method.

Razor the leader butt to a small, hairlike spike. Then, place this narrowed point through the eye of a needle. Cut a short section of bright orange fly line about one inch long and insert the needle right through this short section. With a pair of pliers draw the needle and monofilament through and then attach the leader to the line with your favorite nail or needle knot. You'll have a bright "indicator" that can ride against the knot and is very visible.

Some other approaches utilize cork or styrofoam as strike indicators and these seem to work well also. A few lines are now being made with brightly colored ends, but I've found that contrast obtained by a short indicator is best for me. Also, the Cortland Line Co. has recently introduced *Striker* (which sounds like a wonderfully appropriate name) and I've used this satisfactorily. It is a very visible tab with an adhesive back that can be pinched on the leader or line-leader junction. It is light weight and doesn't seem to interfere with casting or presentation. Finally, a bit of bright polypropylene yarn can be greased and tied in at the line-leader junction or on a leader knot.

Very often an emerger or floating nymph is effective. Depending on the stream, approaches are up and across, cross-stream slack-line casts, or down and across. If there is a singular fish which can only be approached from directly above, a slack line cast fed straight down may be productive as well.

The late Lew Oatman was a well-known subsurface fly expert who developed several popular streamers. On the lower Battenkill in Vermont and New York he often worked nymphs on long, cross-stream, slack line casts with telling effect.

The concept of streamer and bucktail fishing is baitfish simulation. Many anglers swim streamers and bucktails in early season or during rising water periods during the season and let it go at that. Yet, there is season-long effectiveness here as baitfish make up a goodly portion of the diet, especially

*The ubiquitous sculpin is a favorite trout food and serves as the model for a number of effective fly patterns.*

*The Keel Fly concept can be very valuable, not only for surface flies, but various subsurface wets, nymphs, and streamers as well.*

as fish become larger, more secretive, and devote less and less time to surface fedding. Streamer specialist Oatman contended that a great deal of the trout's diet in midsummer consisted of small fish. Many numphs matured during late spring and early summer and left the stream with very small numphs in their early instars, which resulted in the trout searching out small baitfish. He favored his Darter and Grizzly streamers on #8 and #10 long shank hooks and handled them in three basic variations. The first was to cast across stream and retrieve quickly, skittering the fly along near the surface in choppy and turbulent stream sections. the second method was to cast across and allow the fly to swing, moving the rod tip from side to side and recovering line in jerks and darts. In deep holes and placid stretches, the streamer was allowed to sink deep, twitched, and allowed to sink again in an attempt to suggest a wounded minnow that would roll, rest, and recover in a struggling way.

Another specialist, the late Larry Koller, contended the best single approach for the larger fish of his favorite Catskill waters was to cast just above and past the suspected lie of the trout, then retrieve rapidly with a high held rod to keep the fly well up towards the surface.

The Bucktail or a "looks like a lot of things muddler" can also be cast well upstream and across, and brought down in a combination of alternate dead drift and spasmodic twitching motion.

The dry fly is the favored method for most anglers. You can experience the thrill of seeing the strike. When no fish are showing and the angler is "searching" the stream, the usual approach is upstream and across near suspected cover and holding lies. If the fish are rising to a particular fly, any artifical should be close in shape, size, color, and manner of movement. Dries can also be fished in any direction. Cross-stream, slack-line casts, cross and downstream casts and even directly downstream floats are all effective. The real point of any method is to think about the best casting angle from which a cast can be accurately delivered, and to have the fly acting in a natural manner as it passes the fish.

Many anglers delight in studying aquatic life. Yet, all experienced anglers know very capable fishermen who know the difference between the various orders such as mayflies, stoneflies, caddis flies, etc. and more or less let it go at that. Without exception, however, these anglers are observant and respectful of the trout and his senses. They "match" the activity in the sense that if they see a cream colored, half inch long mayfly floating dead with the current, they select their fly on that basis. They may not be very concerned with the difference between *Ephemerella rotunda* and *Ephemerella invaria*, but they still catch fish. In effect, learning about aquatic life is valuable and interesting, but it is not always required for success.

As a starting point for the dry fly angler, it is best to have a variety of types. Most insects run to shades of gray, tan to brown, cream to ginger, and various olive hues. The quick, turbulent stream sections functionally call for high-floating, visible patterns, whereas the medium to slow currents require greater realism in shape, size, color and manner of movement. A basic starting point

*Large Labrador Brook Trout that responded to "twitched" dry fly approach.*

selection might include a few standard divided-wing patterns, no-hackle, and parachutes, a couple of sparse spiders or variants, midges and appropriate terrestrials. Add a couple of caddis imitations and perhaps a bivisible, hair-wing, or hair-body type for the quick stretches. Supplement these with locally popular flies, and there should be an appropriate fly type to deal with most requirements.

Finally, everyone who scribbles about the outdoors must resort to the inevitable cliché from time to time. I've never heard, for instance, of any outdoorsman taking to the trail, lifting the gun or fishing rod without first being duly fortified by "the hearty breakfast." The thought of heading out on nothing more than a piece of toast, juice, and coffee is apparently unthinkable. Another cliché is: **experiment!** When standard approaches don't work, try the offbeat: vary casting angles, retrieve speeds, depths, fly types; use bright attractor flies rather than the duller, more natural types; twitch and skim dries across the surface rather than dead drift them. The basic premise is always to feed the fish, but when that doesn't seem to work, some of the offbeat approaches may. So, even if it is a bit trite, do it: **experiment!**

# 16.

# SPINNING

Spinning is a versatile and effective method that is well-suited to the desires of many backpacking anglers. The basics of equipment handling are learned more easily than is the case with either bait casting or fly fishing. However, this comparative ease is deceptive since expertise with spin gear, like any other method, ultimately demands complete familiarity with the equipment, its capabilities and limitations.

The backcountry spin angler has two general classifications of tackle to consider. Although various manufacturers devise their own descriptive nomenclatures, we can arbitrarily establish our own definitions.

The first, and most versatile, consideration would be a general purpose, light spin outfit geared primarily to one quarter ounce lures. In a standard, two-piece rod this typically consists of a six, six and a half, or seven foot model and a lightweight, open-faced spin reel spooled with four pound monofilament. Since there is no inertia to overcome at the beginning of the cast, such an outfit is fully capable of handling lures both lighter and heavier than one quarter ounce. Instinctively these specs suggest compatibility with medium to large streams as well as ponds and lakes. For many anglers there is no reason to look any further. On the other hand, while it's not really akin to burning down the forest to cook the turkey, such an outfit may be overcalibrated for some more specialized uses.

Some anglers delight in peeking and poking along the mini-creeks where delicately presented, tiny lures are called for. Even at low-water levels on larger streams the so-called ultra-lite approach may be most effective. Slightly scaled down versions of the standard gear are most productive then; sensitive sticks four and one half to six feet long, tiny reels spooled with two or three pound mono and lures of $\frac{1}{16}$ of an ounce, give or take a bit. The little reels can, of course, be spooled with heavier line on occasion, but basically this ultra-light outfit is for the little intimate waters and demands low water conditions on the larger streams.

*At 6.5 oz. with a fast 5 to 1 retrieve ratio, the Orvis 50A spin reel handles lines from 2 to 6 lbs. test. Such a reel is well suited to the backpacker/angler.*

The ultimate choice is an individual one depending on where and when you will be traveling. Some insight into equipment needs will surface as you do the pre-trip planning. You should have a good idea of the type and size of the streams and ponds you will encounter as well as their seasonal water levels.

There are a variety of rods to choose from with glass and graphite dominating the current market. Both materials make excellent spin sticks, but glass has the advantage of excellent knockabout durability at a lower cost. Both materials are available in standard, two-piece models as well as the occasional multi-sectioned, three- or four-piece models. There is also a relatively new five foot, five-piece glass rod with matching mini-size reel from Daiwa. This Daiwa *Minimite* system is expressly designed for the backpacking angler. It comes self-contained in a tough plastic case that is only about fifteen inches long. In spite of the five-piece breakdown, the action of the rod is surprisingly good. It handles a wide range of lure weights, including the one quarter ounce sizes, very well. It certainly deserves consideration from the backpacker looking for one outfit to cover a number of situations with a minimum of gear. In general the two-piece rods are standard, but the careful builder today can provide excellent multi-sectioned models that combine pleasing power to weight ratios, good handling characteristics and sensitivity. It wasn't too many years ago that, with a couple of notable exceptions, the multi-sectioned spin rods offered were worthless, insensitive as a tax collector, and more suited to pole vaulting than plugging. The disappointing aspect of many offerings was the fact that they often came from established firms with a historical significance that would indicate they should have known better. Fortunately, most of these have been redesigned; current pack spin rods are generally very good. To be on the safe side, check them carefully. Enlist the aid of a competent local dealer if you're unfamiliar with the feel of well-designed equipment.

In the standard, two-piece offerings of six to seven foot light rods, you will probably find satisfaction with a moderately fast action rod with most of the bend occuring near the tip. When selecting an ultra-light stick, try to find something a bit slower overall; that is, flexing a bit more into the butt section with a less pronounced tip action. The matching mini-lures used with this rod don't create much resistance to bend so the slower overall recoil characteristics are more desirable for casting ease and accuracy. In pack rod selection, be just as demanding of a good "feel." The use of a pack rod implies you are seeking as much convenience and versatility as possible from one outfit. With proper design and up-to-date ferrule arrangements, some of the pack rods have a feel virtually indistinguishable from a standard, two-piece rod. For all-purpose use, a pack rod that approaches a moderately fast action without undue butt section stiffness should do the job nicely.

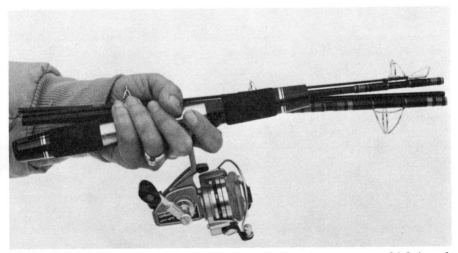

*The Daiwa* Minimite *System packs completely into its own case which is only about 15 inches long. The rod is a 5 foot, 5 inch piece model that has proven to be both convenient to pack and versatile in use.*

# Casting

Casting with a spin outfit is a mechanical delight. The weight of the outgoing lure pulls line from the spool, and the spool remains stationary during the cast. Since there is no inertia to overcome at the beginning of the cast, the spin reel allows the use of very lightweight lures. As a result of this casting principle, the new angler may acquire the fundamentals of spin tackle handling in a fraction of the time required for equal facility with other methods such as a bait casting rod or even a fly rod.

The normal casting stroke is the overhand cast, useful at all times unless streamside obstructions dictate a different casting plane. The usual rod grip places the reel foot between the middle and ring fingers although the size of your hand may make a different placement more comfortable. The thumb lies along the top of the cork grip. The rod and forearm should be in a straight line, aimed at the desired target. The upper arm is comfortably close to, but not jammed tightly, against the body, Disengage the pickup bail with your free hand and lift the line free, supporting it on the ball of your index finger. Begin the casting stroke by smoothly pivoting off the elbow, lifting the casting hand to about eye level. When the forearm and rod reach a vertical position, stop. The weight of the lure flexes the rod to the rear. Bring the rod smoothly down and forward, reversing the original path traveled, releasing line as the rod approaches its starting position. There is a slight wrist emphasis at the top of

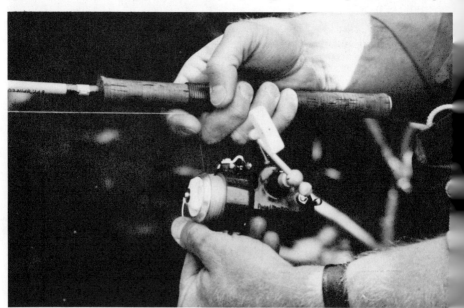

*Support the line on the ball of the index finger. Open the bail in preparatio.*
*for the cast.*

the backstroke and at the end of the forward stroke.

About the only potential problem is the correct forward release point; releasing too early will send the lure sailing skyward, too late will sent it crashing into the water at your feet. A few trials and you'll be on the right track. You may, in fact, be pleasantly surprised when the lure sails out for excellent distance.

It's time now to face the reality of backcountry spinning. On the small to medium-sized streams, distance usually is not too important. Reasonable accuracy and lure control are more important. Backpacking and angling have enough inherent problems without introducing the need for tree climbing agility to retrieve artlessly flung lures dangling twenty feet above the pool in some ancient spruce tree. The key to accuracy and lure control is the index finger of the rod hand. With the lure in flight you can slow its speed to prevent overcasting the target by bringing the forefinger back towards the spool, creating

*Bruce Bowlen demonstrates various casts*

*Aim the rod at desired target. Disengage the pickup bail and support the line on the ball of the index finger.*

*Pivot off the elbows, elevating the hand to the eye/ear level. Stop as forearm and rod attain the vertical. Lure weight flexes rod to the rear.*

117

*Reverse the original path with a smooth, fluid motion.*

*Line is released as the hand approaches the original, starting position.*

friction against the outgoing line. The lure can be stopped completely by simply touching the spool rim with the forefinger. Spend some time in your practice sessions to ensure automatic responses from the index finger. It pays off in restricted quarters.

If streamside obstructions prevent the usual overhand casting stroke, work in sidearm or backhand planes. You can also use an underhanded tossing motion for moderate distance in very confined quarters. Still another possibility when really walled in is the bow and arrow cast. A cautious note accompanies the use of this cast: Be wary of those sharp hook points in preparing for and completing this cast.

*Sidearm and backhand casts are practical when obstructions prevent the usual overhand stroke.*

*In really hemmed-in areas try the Bow and Arrow cast. Carefully grasp treble hooks and draw rod into circular bow. Lure-holding hand is about at a hip pocket level.*

*Then release lure, and cushion forward stroke by slightly elevating the rod hand as the lure begins its forward flight.*

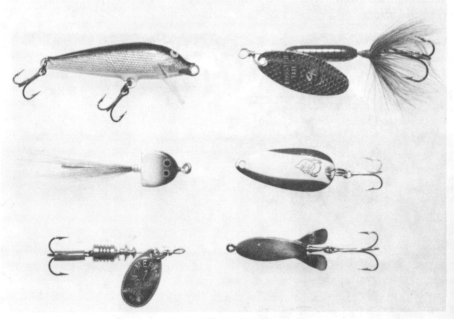

*Representative Spinning Lure Types:*

1. Rapala plug
2. Wiggle Jig
3. Mepps spinner
4. Rooster Tail Spinner
5. Red and White spoon
6. Swiss spinner

# 17.

# BASIC FLY CASTING

Fly casting is mechanically less efficient than spinning. The spin lure represents a concentrated weight mass. As the spin rod swings forward the lure speeds on its way, pulling the trailing monofilament. In contrast, a fly is virtually weightless and cannot contribute to the cast. The burden of casting weight is in the fly line, distributed over those several feet of line extended beyond the rod tip. In effect, a spin lure makes the outgoing flight possible; a fly simply goes along for the outgoing ride, taken there by the unrolling and extending fly line.

Despite these differences, there are similarities in the basic casting strokes. Normal fly casting is relatively simple. There are only a few things to do right, everything else just complicates the learning process. The more practice sessions that can be arranged, the more rapid the progress. Assuming, of course, the correct motions are the ones that are practiced. The early sessions are best done on water if it is at all possible. The surface tension of water assists in the initial line-pickup motions. If water is unavailable, an open lawn will do almost as well. On moving water face downstream, strip off about twenty feet of line and allow it to drift downstream with the current. If practicing on the lawn select an open area of about forty or fifty feet. Stand in the middle as you require both backcast and forward cast space.

Throughout the discussions, the terms rod hand and line hand will be used so the instructions will be clear for both right-handed and left-handed casters. Initially, only the rod hand will be required. Begin by securing the fly line under the rod hand forefinger or hand itself, clamping it to the cork grip so it can't creep out. We want to work with a fixed line length for the moment. The premise is that the forearm, wrist, and hand will act primarily as a continuation of the rod through most of the casting cycle with the elbow as the major pivot point of the cast. The wrist will come into play briefly (but importantly) as a secondary pivotal point in both the top of the backcast and the end of the forward cast.

The grip on the corks should be comfortably firm with the thumb lying atop the grip, pointing down the rod. In the beginning sessions open up the rod side foot a bit. That is, a right-handed caster should stand facing the target area, the left foot facing straight ahead and placed slightly in advance of the right foot which is angled outward slightly, a position which permits turning the head easily to visually follow the rear line extensions of the backcast. Left-handers: reverse the procedure. The upper arm is close to the body, the elbow is separated from the body by a comfortable couple of inches. The forearm, wrist and hand now act as a continuation of the rod which is angled down slightly, the tip pointing toward the water. The stance is comfortable and the rod-side foot is sustaining most of the body weight.

The conventional cast is an overhand movement: Begin with a smooth, progressive, lifting motion, pivoting off the elbow with the wrist and hand held almost stiffly. This permits the entire rod to contribute effectively to the cast. With the short line you are working with, the end of the fly line and the upper part of the leader (butt section) may leave the water. Only the remainder of the leader is still in the surface film. Speeding up progressively, the hand raises toward eye level. As the rod approaches a vertical there is some wrist emphasis towards the rear. Tighten the squeeze on the grip with the thumb and index finger at this point and the rod should stop at the proper angle. The thumb is about vertical, or just slightly past vertical, and the rod is angled up and back. Turn your head to follow the rear line extension. Just before the unrolling "U" shape straightens out completely, begin the forward delivery of the cast.

In due time it won't be necessary to turn and watch the flow of the backcast; the feel and timing will become instinctive. However, most new casters learn to coordinate the timing of the movements easiest if they watch as well as try to feel the tugging line snuggling nicely against the rod in a proper backcast. The forward cast is a "path reversal." The forearm, hand and wrist are almost stiff and drive the rod butt progressively forward and down. As the rod starts to turn over in the front, the wrist and thumb come into play to emphasize the forward stroke. The cast is finished with the rod pointing straight ahead, just about parallel to the water. The line and leader should unroll completely in the air, extend fully and drop gently to the surface.

Try for smooth power application and the proper timing of the movements. Many new casters take extreme actions; some tend to handle the equipment too gently, thus failing to develop the required bend in the rod which will assist in obtaining the nice, flowing, back-and-forth motions of a good cast. Others try to overpower the equipment and apply strength in short, jerky bursts. Again, it's proper timing and smooth power application that will do the job most pleasantly and most efficiently.

Make this fundamental cast several times. Each one should be a complete

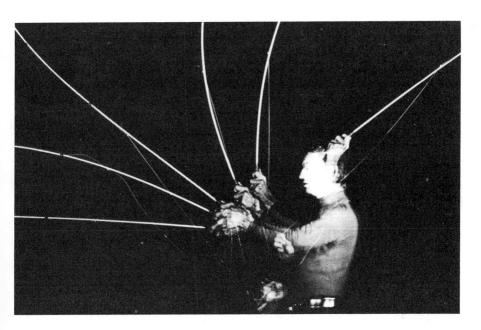

*The average length, forward casting cycle in stroboscopic sequence. The hand is about at eye/ear level with the rod angled up and back of vertical. The hand pushes forward and down until a late wrist and thumb emphasis is introduced to bring the rod about parallel with the water.*

---

cycle of pickup, backcast, forward cast, and delivery of the fly to the water. Try to make each cast better and smoother than the one previously. Rapid progress is possible if the practice sessions are handled correctly.

It is also important to realize the role of the backcast. New hands often minimize the importance of the backcast, placing most of their effort into the forward delivery. Nevertheless, if the backcast is properly formed, the forward cast is almost automatic. Tame the backcast first and everything else will fall into place quickly. Some find the concepts easier if they begin to work the rod in a sidearm motion, rather than overhead. Just alter the plane of the cast to a sidearm motion. The line loops will form and unroll more or less parallel to the ground. The line flow and the timing are easily watched and the importance of smoothly coordinated movements becomes quickly apparent. When this sidearming motion is under control, just change the angle of the cast, working back up into the normal overhead or vertical path.

The wrist is held almost stiffly through most, but not all of the motions. There is wrist emphasis at the top of the backcast and the end of the forward cast. The beginner's danger tends to be a slack wrist at the top of the backcast, angling the rod too far back, perhaps with the tip section pointed to the ground or water behind. Experienced hands say that the line follows the rod. What you do with the rod tip is reflected in the flow of the line a moment later. Therefore, watch the backcast and don't allow the rod to angle further back than it should. At the top of a well-delivered backcast, the rod hand is automatically placed in a position from which it is ready to drive forward into a nice delivery cast. The end of the forward cast is delivered with some wrist emphasis to bring the rod

*The Basic Casting Cycle: (Landy Bartlett demonstrates) Begin the backcast by angling the rod low, with the tip pointing toward the water. Be sure to remove all slack line. Next, the forearm is elevated smoothly until only the leader remains on the surface of the water. This ensures the whole rod is lifting the line into the backcast. The line-holding hand simply maintains a light tension on the line.*

*At the top of the motion an easy wrist snap to the rear allows the line to float up and back toward the required line extension. The casting hand is about at the eye/ear level and the line-holding hand is still maintaining light tension.*

he original path is reversed as the casting hand drives smoothly and progres-
*vely* forward and down to terminate in a decisive wrist and thumb power
*oplication*. The line-holding hand is still maintaining tension. Some three
*et* of line exist behind it and lead to the fly reel.

*he* rod is stopped about parallel to the water. The unrolling fly line and leader
*ill* extend completely in the air and drop gently to the water. Note that the
*ack* line that existed behind the line-holding hand is being allowed to shoot
*to* the cast, pulled by the outgoing taper.

---

most parallel to the water.

Another cast which helps to make the correct motions clear is the roll cast.
*ater* is required for smooth execution of the roll cast. On the lawn the line

tends to slide along ineffectually. Use the rod hand only, clamping the fly line to the cork grip so it can't creep out. It is vital to form this cast slowly, elevating the rod and tilting it slightly to the outside of the body so the rod and line lie in different planes and don't tangle on the forward cast portion of the cycle. A belly of line will form from the rod tip to the water. Allow this line belly to pass behind the elbow and come to a complete stop. Now, drive the rod hand ahead and down in a normal, forward casting motion, applying the casting power progressively and ending the cast with a short, decisive wrist and thumb power application. The rod should finish almost parallel to the water at the termination of the cast. About the only problems that may arise tend to do so for one of two reasons: first, the line must be brought into position quite slowly; secondly, the line must be allowed to stop for a brief second before the start of the forward stroke.

When these one-handed fundamentals are in good order, introduce the other hand, the line hand, to the movements. Even as a fundamental, the line hand role is very important, maintaining line control and tension. New casters tend to minimize its importance and are understandably fascinated by the rod motion. However, the line-hand role is vitally important to all fly casting. When advanced line hauling techniques become important, the line hand is just about as busy as the rod hand.

Strip an additional four or five feet of line from the reel and let it hang loosely from the butt guide, sagging back to the reel. Reach up to grasp the line between thumb and forefinger, letting the line lay loosely over the fingers. The line hand should now be at a comfortable distance to the side of the rod hand with the line coming directly from the butt guide to the hand under light tension. The belly of slack line now exists behind the line hand and sags back down and up to the reel. As the normal backcast is made, the line hand maintains light tension and is allowed to drift slightly across the body and up a bit essentially following the path of the rod hand so that an equal distance between the hands is maintained during the whole cycle. On the forward delivery cast the line can be fed through the line holding hand as the momentum of the outgoing taper pulls it for a slight extra shoot. Functionally, this line hand assures line control and maintains tension. Moving it to follow behind the rod hand places it in a position where it is available to introduce a well-coordinated pull of its own when the rod is coming forward to increase line speed and provide extra distance through the "shooting" of slack line. In a very real sense the line hand also aids accuracy in normal casting. If the line is fed consistently through the line hand, it is, as we've mentioned, under control. Closing the hand slightly when the line is on its outgoing forward flight slows the line somewhat. Pinching the line between the thumb and fingers stops the line over its target. Therefore, it is quite easy to cast with a bit more power than is required to reach a specific target area and then stop the line in flight over the designated area to drop the fly just where you want it.

The false casting cycle is a necessary procedure with multiple uses. Your accuracy is improved by lining up the flight of the line with the specific target area. It dries a floating fly as excess water droplets are shaken from the fly during the back and forth motions. When coordinated with the line hand, false casts can help build up additional line speed to combat head winds or help shoot the line for extra distance. The procedure is essentially an incomplete forward cast. Stop the rod high on the forward stroke, as opposed to the parallel delivery cast position, and the line will begin to straighten in the air. Just before it reaches a complete forward extension, bring it back into another backcasting motion. When the delivery cast is to be made, allow the line to fully straighten to the rear. Catch it as the line weight snuggles against the rod and

*The false cast is an incomplete forward casting motion, checked with the rod at a high angle, allowing the line to almost completely extend forward in the air before being brought back into another backcast. False casts allow you to get out more line without disturbing the water, and also dry off dry flies.*

---

drive forward to finish with the usual smooth wrist emphasis and final rod turnover.

Although the usual stroke is overhead, that sidearm cast we looked at briefly is a valuable move on the stream. With shy fish we can often make close approaches by crouching and moving slowly and casting from a sidearm position to minimize the chance of the flashing rod being seen by the cautious trout.

*An underpowered side-arm cast will produce a curve to the right as the line has insufficient power and speed to attain the normal straight line extension.*

*An overpowered side-arm cast, especially if it is checked abruptly by a vigorou throwing-in motion of the rod tip and assisted at the same time by a slig line-hand tug, will hook past a straight line extension and fall in a curve your left.*

Sidearm casts also help drive a fly under low hanging foliage. Furthermore, they allow modifications in our timing to introduce curves into the presentation. There are other curve cast methods, but the principle behind the curves is best understood if we examine the line flow of a sidearm cast. Any cast, no matter the angle of origin (overhead, sidearm, or backhand) extends in a straight line if the timing is correct. When casting sidearm, the line loops form more or less parallel to the water. A correctly executed cast extends forward in a straight line. However, if the forward stroke is underpowered, the line fails to attain the straight line and falls to the water in a curve to your right—if you are right handed. An overpowered sidearm cast, especially if it is checked abruptly in flight by a slight line hand tug, hooks around past our straight line and falls in a curve to the left.

Slack line casts are often advantageous to improve a float or drift, to contend with mixed and conflicting currents, or to work a fly directly downstream in such a manner that the fly moves with the current flow seemingly unrestrained by line or leader influence. One possibility is the "S" cast. This is formed by taking advantage of the fundamental that whatever is done to the rod during the cast will be reflected in the flow of the line a moment later. Allow the backcast to straighten to the rear in the normal manner. As the rod moves into the forward stroke, wiggle it from side to side. The line passing through the guides is influenced by the side-to-side rod movements and extends and drops onto the water in a series of wiggles or "S" shapes. This action can be controlled easily be varying the number and size of the curves that are formed. A few firm, widely spaced wiggles of the rod produce a few deep curves; a series of quicker, shorter, side-to-side rod movements produce a larger number of smaller curves.

There are some alternative motions to introduce slack into the cast. To keep much of the slack near the fly, make the cast with insufficient power to fully straighten out. This is actually a slightly underpowered normal cast. Some casters prefer a forward stroke made with greater emphasis than is needed to reach the target. At the end of the forward motion a slight pull back is made. This causes the speeding line to bounce back and drop in a series of slack curves. Still another alternative is the parachute cast. On the final forward delivery start the rod ahead and stop it abruptly while it is still vertical. Don't follow through on the forward stroke. The rod hand moves from a position opposite your ear straight ahead for about eighteen inches; then it is abruptly checked. Immediately lower the rod hand about a foot and the incomplete forward stroke will yank the line and leader backward. It will fall loosely to the water. On a direct downstream drift, the rod can then be brought to a position parallel to the water and more line can be pulled from the reel and shaken out of the guides to extend a long drift.

The cast with the greatest distance potential is the double haul. Despite the fact that you will be attempting longer distance casts, the key elements remain smoothness and proper timing of the rod hand and line hand. Since there are more motions involved, practice with more than the usual amount of line extended beyond the rod tip.

Lay out some thirty five or forty feet of line. Strip another twenty feet of line from the reel and allow it to drop loosely at your feet. The grip on the rod is a bit firmer than usual. Lean forward a little to extend the line hand towards the butt or first guide and grasp the line firmly between the thumb and forefinger. Begin moving the line towards you a split second before the rod begins to lift. This starts the line moving towards you and helps to power the line into a smooth backcast. The hands now work in opposing directions: The line hand sweeps down and back heading for a hip pocket position, while the rod hand moves up and back towards a strong backcast position. The hands are momentarily separated. Now, as the backcast begins to extend to the rear, the line hand (still holding the line in the same relative position) moves up and across the body towards the rod hand. With the backcast straight out behind the rod, the line hand starts a smooth accelerating movement back towards the hip pocket position and the rod hand drives ahead. A decisive wrist and thumb delivery complete the rod turnover and the line hand releases its grip on the line. The outgoing taper pulls the extra slack through the guides for a long forward line extension.

If the single cycle isn't enough to gain the desired distance or line speed, simply false cast a time or two and then release the line for the final shoot.

Although the double haul is definitely the big water, long distance cast, the principle is valuable with any tackle. On small streams just a slight tug of the line hand helps overcome the surface tension and move the line into a nice backcast. A tiny pull with the line hand while coming forward can shoot a line for extra yardage or help compensate for a sudden puff of headwind.

The double haul can be done with the double taper or the weight forward line, but many anglers who must habitually reach way out prefer the shooting head. This is a short, usually thirty foot fly line section, attached to one hundred feet of twenty to twenty-five pound monofilament or a specially made small diameter level fly line. Conventional backing line fills the remainder of the reel. Anglers working with shooting heads have devised some unique methods of handling the loose running line behind the "head." Some rig paper clips or clothespins to their wader tops on which to hang the coils. Some hold the loose coils in their mouth and open their mouth on the forward cast to let the line soar away. Some anglers prefer the shooting basket to handle the retrieved line, stripping it into the basket to be shot forward on the subsequent cast.

From the standpoint of handling the head while casting, there are two points worthy of mention. Keep the shooting head close to the rod tip. If the head is too far from the rod tip, the light monofilament cannot support it properly. If it is too close to the rod tip, the connection between the head and the mono may be pulled into the tip top and interfere with the smoothness of the motions. Work with it a while to find the correct overhang for you. Usually something between two and six feet is appropriate. Next, on the final forward stroke release the cast earlier or aimed higher than normal since there is less friction in the guides to slow its flight. It will turn over too fast otherwise.

The wind is an obvious fact of angling. It can come at you from any angle. When it's brisk enough, it must be compensated for.

With a strong wind from the rear, it's best to begin with a strong horizontal line pickup supplemented by a short, smooth line-hand pull. The rod angle is essentially the same as employed in a usual sidearming cast which keeps the line low where there may be less wind resistance. Turn your head to watch the unrolling loop. As it straightens, immediately start a looping overhand forward stroke. There is no pause in the whole cycle. The backcast and forward cast planes are widely separated and there is no danger of them tangling. The line weight nestles continuously against the rod and the whole motion is a smooth, continuous oval which starts to the side and sweeps up and overhead with the forward cast aimed higher than normal to take advantage of the following wind.

The on-coming headwind is only a problem of velocity. There's no problem in getting a smooth backcast as it is wind assisted. The key to defeating or contending with the headwind lies in a smooth, strong, accelerating forward delivery. A line hand pull at the time the rod turns over helps throw a tight, narrow loop into the wind. The rod turnover is delayed as long as possible. The idea is to keep the line driving tight and close to the water.

Crosswinds offer the potential hazard of having the fly driven right at you. Ideally the rod is always on the downwind side. If, for example, you are right handed, the wind that blows from left to right is no problem. Everything is safely away from your body. the wind crossing from right to left is more dangerous. Compensations may depend on the wind velocities. If the breezes aren't too strong and gusty, a strong sidecasting motion will probably be sufficient. Stronger winds call for different measures. One possibility is to alter the normal casting planes. If you are righthanded, make the backcast with the rod tilted away slightly to the right and keep the rod hand high as the backcast unrolls to the rear. As you come forward alter the plane of the forward stroke and bring your hand virtually overhead. The line will ride high and pass safely to your left. Or, use the backhand cast. Start by holding the rod in the usual manner, but angled toward the downwind side. That is, a righthanded caster with a wind blowing from right to left would angle the rod across the body and to the left. The pickup is made off the elbow, assisted by a short line-hand tug. The rod angles up over your left shoulder. The backcast unrolls safely downwind and you are ready for the forward stroke. Move ahead with the usual stiffish forearm drive, assisted by the ending wrist and thumb emphasis. A smooth line-hand tug on the forward cast will help pull in extra speed if it is needed.

There are some variations of the usual line pickup that can be helpful on the stream. The norm is a smoothly accelerating motion up and back. With a long line extended, a short line-hand pull helps to coordinate with the lifting rod to power into the firm and decisive backcast that's needed. Apart from these usual considerations there are a couple other possibilities. One is the roll cast pickup. Dry fly anglers normally face the current and work the fly back close to their position. The roll pickup saves time and is very easy to execute. As the line

*The Roll Cast permits a forward line extension when the caster is hemmed in by obstacles to the rear. Begin by slowly elevating the rod, tilting it slightly to the outside of the body so the rod and line lie in different planes and won't tangle on the forward cast portion of the cycle. A belly of line will form from the rod tip to the water. Allow this to pass behind the elbow and come to a complete stop. Then, drive the rod hand ahead and down in a normal casting motion, applying the casting power smoothly and progressively and ending with a decisive wrist and thumb power application. The rod should be about parallel to the water at the termination of the cast. Be sure that the line is brought into position slowly, and allow the line to stop momentarily before beginning the forward cycle.*

*The roll cast pickup is commonly employed by upstream-directed anglers. It is also useful with sinking lines and shooting heads to lift these airborne with a minimum of fuss. As the belly of slack forms outside the rod-side shoulder, briskly snap the rod forward with an incomplete roll casting motion. The moving loop will pick line, leader and fly off the water and into the air, where a standard backcast can be made.*

---

drifts back, elevate the rod slowly, tilting it outside and allow the line loop to form outside your elbow. Start the rod forward but do not follow through. Stop the rod with the butt angled about 45° above the water. A moving loop forms to pick line, leader, and fly off the water and into the air. Now a normal backcasting motion can be made. This pickup also works very well with sinking lines and shooting heads.

The snap pickup accomplishes much the same thing as the roll pickup. Bring the rod towards an eleven o'clock position. Then make a quick wrist snap, stopping the rod at about ten o'clock. A running curve moves down the line and kicks the fly upward and into position for the backcast. This lifting pickup, as opposed to one that draws the line across the surface, is very useful in avoiding obstructions or surface weeds. The fly doesn't have to be drawn into the weeds where it may hang up.

The switch or zig-zag pickup is one more way to avoid obstacles. This motion forces a series of moving curves into the line to lift the fly into the air. Hold the rod forward, angled slightly down toward the water. Then move the rod firmly from side to side while you elevate the arm. By the time the rod tip is between ten and eleven o'clock the fly should have left the surface and a normal backcast can be made.

When you are actually fishing, the forefinger of the rod hand will act almost as another rod guide. After the cast settles on the water, you want to be in a correct position to strike the fish. Most anglers place the line over the forefinger of the rod hand or between thumb and forefinger of the rod hand. All retrieves or line manipulations are done behind this grip to assure a quick, slack free response to a taking fish. There are a number of retrieve variations. The easiest is to form coils of line in the line hand. Gather in the first loop well back in the hand. Place the next loop slightly forward of this. Hold the last gathered loop in place by the thumb and forefinger. Line can be released to an outgoing cast in an orderly manner without snags.

Generally speaking, fish should be played off the reel. Small fish are sometimes just stripped in, but all desirable fish demand being handled off the reel. If there is a great deal of slack when the fish takes, it can be slipped under the index finger of the rod hand as the fish makes his initial run while, at the same time, the balance of the slack line is being reeled in. With all the slack taken up, the rod is elevated and the fish goes where he will, but runs off the reel. When you can recover line, do so by reeling in.

Netting a tired fish isn't difficult. Unfortunately, they often have something left. Many a fish has been lost at this last critical moment. Submerge the net and bring the fish in head first. If the head of the trout is held high, he won't see the net. Then slack the line so the fish will naturally turn into the net meshes and lift him free.

# 18.

# EQUIPMENT COVERAGE

## Fly Lines

To lay the groundwork for any fly line discussion, we should get the terminology in order and comprehend the current line rating system. Since 1961 a fly line rating based on weight has been in effect. The weight factor around which the system revolves is the grain: $437\frac{1}{2}$ grains equal one ounce. The committee from the American Fishing Tackle Manufacturers Association which formulated the ratings further concluded the average length cast to be 30 feet, so the system is concerned only with the first 30 feet of line, exclusive of any taper tip. The grain weights for various lines were given numerical designations from 1 through 12 (although some special purpose heavier lines have since come into being), and the weights range from 60 grains (a #1 line) to 380 grains (a #12 line) plus or minus acceptable manufacturing tolerances. Prefixes were established to designate taper type: L for level line; DT for double taper; WF for weight forward; and ST for single taper or shooting head. Letters indicate line function: F for floating line; S for sinking line; I for intermediate, a line which has a specific gravity about that of water. When dressed the intermediate line can serve as a floating line. Without treatment it serves as a slow sinking line. Lastly, F/S indicates a floating-sinking type such as the popular sinktip lines where the 10 feet of line at the end sinks while the balance of the line floats. There are other versions of this concept with 20 or 30 foot forward sinking sections.

When taken in combination, the system tells us taper type, weight and function, e.g., DT5F is a double taper 5 weight (140 grains) floater, a WF5S is a weight forward 5 weight (140 grains) sinking line and a WF5F/S would be a weight forward 5 weight (140 grains) floating-sinking line in which the forward section of the line sinks while the balance floats.

There is rarely any need for the average angler to be concerned with the actual grain weights. The simple numerical designations are usually adequate information. About the only confusion that may arise occurs when looking at the sinking lines. Available technology permits the line makers to vary the specific gravity of the line coatings to achieve differing sink rates from quite slow to very fast. Since the AFTMA ratings do not take this into account, the manufacturers further identify their various sinking lines by labeling the product with an indication of the relative sinking speed. For example, the Cortland Line Company offers their Type 1 slow sinker, Type 2 fast sinker, Type 3 extra fast sinker and their Type 4 super sinker. Another leading line manufacturer, Scientific Anglers, varies the terminology but also offers sinking lines of four densities. Beyond this there are some special cases where a lead core line may be set up as a shooting taper system for really deep work. About all we can tell at the moment is that a specific line from a given maker will sink slower or faster than a different sinking line from the same maker. Perhaps in time there will be a specific standard established, but in truth the lack of such a standard is no hindrance. The line makers identify the relative sinking rates, and the specific gravity information is usually available. There's no problem in sorting out the suitable sinking line for your requirements.

Despite some specialized loose ends, the line rating system supplies the essential information and greatly simplifies line-to-rod relationships. Virtually all rod makers indicate the recommended line weights to use. What remains is the question of function and taper type. For most anglers the first fly line should be a floater. Which then, double taper or weight forward? Within the framework of their design, both are good. The double taper is reversible: As one end wears it can be swapped end for end to provide long term economy. At short and medium distances the double taper does well everything asked of it, be it roll casting, delicate presentation, or whatever. But, the arguments go, so does a well-designed forward taper. Some makers in fact run tapers that are identical for the first 30 feet so there is little to choose between the two line types where these average requirements are concerned. However, let's say it is necessary to present a fly quickly to a more distant target. You're working with 30 feet of line in the air and a good fish suddenly shows at the 50 foot distance. With a weight forward line the effective pulling weight is out there, beyond the rod tip. When the line is shot on the delivery cast, this advancing, pulling weight tugs along a lighter weight, smaller diameter running line.

By comparison, a double taper with a 30 foot working length of line in the air would be asked to pull a heavier, larger diameter, belly section out of the guides. Thus, the pulling weight of a double taper has more of a frictional load and a greater line weight to overcome. It's also likely that there will be less line speed obtained in a minimum of motions with the double taper, so the caster must apply more power to the cast or work through one or two additional false cast motions.

# LINE RATING
## SYSTEMS

### Symbols

| | | |
|---|---|---|
| L | = | Level |
| DT | = | Double Taper |
| WF | = | Weight Forward |
| ST | = | Single Taper |

### Weights

| # | Wt. | Range |
|---|---|---|
| 1 | 60 | 54 — 66 |
| 2 | 80 | 74 — 86 |
| 3 | 100 | 94 — 106 |
| 4 | 120 | 114 — 126 |
| 5 | 140 | 134 — 146 |
| 6 | 160 | 152 — 168 |
| 7 | 185 | 177 — 193 |
| 8 | 210 | 202 — 218 |
| 9 | 240 | 230 — 250 |
| 10 | 280 | 270 — 290 |
| 11 | 330 | 318 — 342 |
| 12 | 380 | 368 — 392 |

### Types

F = Floating
S = Sinking
I = Intermediate (Floats or Sinks)
F/S = sink tip

Weight in grains based on first 30' of line exclusive of any taper tip:

### Examples:

| DT9S | | DT9F |
|---|---|---|
| Tip | ←——30 ft. 240 grains | Tip | ←——30 ft. 240 grains |

(Note: 437½ grains equal 1 ounce)

*Chart: Courtesy*
*Orvis Co., Inc.*

Profiles and taper dimensions of selected Cortland 333 Tapered lines.

**CORTLAND "333" DOUBLE TAPERS**

DT6F    6"        8'        73' Belly        8'        6"

DT8F    6"        8'        73' Belly        8'        6"

DT9F    6"        8'        73' Belly        8'        6"

**CORTLAND "333" ROCKET TAPERS**

WF5F    6"    12'        18' Belly        6'        68½' Running Line

WF7F    6"    12'        20' Belly        6'        66½' Running Line

WF8F    6"    12'        24' Belly        6'        62½' Running Line

WF9F    6"    16'        26' Belly        6'        56½' Running Line

*Chart: Courtesy Cortland Line Co.*

Another everyday fact of angling life is wind. The weight distribution of the forward taper is a more favorable distribution to contend with such conditions. An overly brief consensus then concludes that when the fishing is done on small, sheltered waters where delicate presentation is the usual requirement, the economy of a double taper is an influencing factor. However, if you need, as many do, the versatility to handle many different circumstances, the weight forward is apt to make the most sense.

The backpacking angler must be weight and space conscious when assembling an outfit. The usual procedure is to select a rod, then a reel and line to go with it. Working backwards in outfit assembly is a more satisfactory arrangement in that it keeps the emphasis on the appropriate line weight. Realistically, the fly size range to be presented determines the leader tippet size, while the physical conditions such as average required casting distance, water clarity, etc., help determine leader length. Then the fly line is the delivery vehicle to carry the fly and help kick the leader over neatly. This line must be of an appropriate weight to satisfy the twin demands of handling the average distance needs and reasonable fly presentation. The rod should be selected by its ability to move the selected line weight efficiently and comfortably. Since virtually every region of the country that offers potential interest to the angler-packer offers a range of possible water types from small sheltered waters up to larger rivers and lakes, versatility is important.

No single outfit does everything equally well. Therefore, a quick look at the inherent functional qualities of various line weights may help establish the best starting point for the individual angler. The very lightweight tapers such as #3 and #4 are ideally suited to small fly presentation over wary fish in demanding conditions. Being so light, however, they may be difficult to handle in the wind. As good as they are for their purpose, they must be regarded as fairly specialized. A #5 weight approaches the better compromise ground, as it expands the range of fly sizes that may be handled easily without sacrificing much in the way of delicate presentation when it's needed. Though it is not the best line weight for beating the breezes or really consistently long casts, it has enough weight to reach a good distance in the hands of a moderately competent caster. The #6 weight is capable of excellent fly presentation and the bonus of a bit more line weight further expands the fly size range and distance potential. There are many anglers who regard this as the line for one rod use. The #7 weight is enough line to handle nicely under breezy conditions. It handles an excellent range of fly sizes and types. Admittedly it's a bit more line weight than one would like for extremely spooky trout in demanding conditions when tiny flies are required, but it is an excellent all purpose line for medium to larger streams and most ponds and lakes. This weight is especially popular in many western areas as the starting point, general purpose trout line. Stepping up to the heavier 8, 9 and 10 weight lines is an implication that the emphasis is on larger flies, large water requirements, and perhaps longer average casting requirements or deeply sunken work with big wets, nymphs, streamers, and bucktails.

Based on this, the starting point for most backpacking anglers will fall in the middle range from the lightish #5 line through the medium weights of 6 and 7. There are so many variables that these suggestions should be modified or reinforced by expert local advice. Your local dealer can discuss your intentions knowingly, and being familiar with the area water types and seasonal imitative problems, he can help you zero in on the specific line weight and corresponding outfit.

On an everyday basis, the angler may head for the stream with a reel and an extra spool rigged with a different line type, or he may even carry two reels fully loaded and ready to interchange quickly. The "spare" equipment weight isn't a consideration in conventional day to day angling. However the backpacker has special problems and is very conscious of weight and space. If it's a weekend trip into a backwoods pond, the overall pack weight shouldn't be excessive. The angler might get by with a reel and an extra spool rigged with a different line type. Longer trips or trips into areas where there is a variety of water types present more problems. The weight of extra reels or even extra spools with all the line types that one might like to have along can be excessive. Fortunately, there is an answer: the shooting taper system.

The typical shooting taper is a short, usually 30 foot, length of fly line which is attached to 100 feet of monofilament or lightweight, small diameter level fly line. This in turn is attached to conventional dacron or micron backing which fills the balance of the reel spool.

The concept is valuable enough for any angler to at least consider for everyday work, but for the backpacking angler it is vital if maximum versatility is to be obtained with a minimum of weight and pack space. The hiker could, for instance, take off to the mountains with a single fly reel and several 30 foot shooting heads such as a floater, a sinktip, a slow sinker, a fast sinker, and an extra fast sinker and still have the whole arrangement weigh less and take up less space than a fly reel with one extra spool. And no matter at what level the fish were working, there would be an appropriate line type available to reach them.

Many shooting heads are available commercially. They can also be easily made up. Cut a conventional fly line 30 feet back from the end. It's most economical to cut a double taper, as two tapered heads and one level head will be obtained. Perhaps an angling buddy will go in on the price of a double taper, giving each of you a tapered head. You can flip a coin for ownership of the level head that remains.

Most commercial heads come with a spliced-in attaching loop. If monofilament is used behind the head, it is commonly clinch-knotted to this loop. To change heads, simply cut the knot and tie on the next head that is to be used. With level fly line you need to splice in a loop. This is connected to the shooting head in a loop to loop junction to form a square knot. To change heads, just unloop the one and loop on the next. These interlocking loops are also used to connect the running line to the backing. They are strong, smooth, and reliable. Your dealer may be able to splice any needed loops, although it's an easy

**FOR ATTACHING FLY TO LEADER . . . .**

The Clinch Knot

**TO MAKE LOOP FOR ATTACHING LEADER BUTT TO FLY LINE . . . .**

The Perfection Knot

1. Thread line through eye.

2. Give line at least five turns around itself, then bring end back through the loop.

3. While holding line end, pull the twists tight up against the eye.

1. Take 1-1/2 turns around the line.

2. Bring end through between the forward and back loops of turn taken in Step 1.

3. The back loop formed in Step 1 is then pulled up through the front loop, and pulled tight.

**TO CONNECT THE SECTIONS OF A TAPERED LEADER . . . . .**

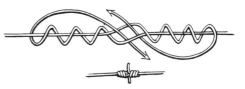

The Turle Knot

1. Thread leader through eye of fly. Then holding an open loop, tie a "Granny" Knot, forming a sliding loop.

2. Bring open loop forward over the fly.

3. Pull on leader 'til loop closes, tight behind the eye of the fly.

The Barrel Knot

1. Give end of line 1 at least three turns around line 2, and bring end back through loop as illustrated.

2. Give end of line 2 same number of turns around line 1 (in reverse rotation) and bring back through loop (in opposite direction).

3. While holding both line ends, pull twists firm and tight against each other. Ends can be trimmed very close, giving a neat smooth knot.

# Basic Fisherman's Knots

procedure and worth doing yourself. One standard reference for this type of information as well as all other angling knots is *Practical Fishing Knots* by two fine angler-authors, Lefty Kreh and Mark Sosin (Crown Publishers, New York).

Behind the shooting head itself there are three possibilities: flattened or oval monofilament, round monofilament, or small diameter level fly line. The flattened mono floats well and may tangle less in normal use than the round mono, but it is susceptible to kinking or twisting. The round mono is very durable and forming knots is slightly easier than in the oval mono, but it may tangle more often. Both types of mono should be kept clean for best handling and longest casting qualities. The use of a silicone conditioner such as *Mono-Slik* from Maxima is recommended. The flotation of the mono will be improved and twist and drag will be reduced. The alternative to either monofilament is a small diameter line marketed as shooting line or the purchase of a lightweight, small diameter level fly line such as a L2F. For the beginner with the shooting head concept, this may be the best arrangement. The casting distance is reduced but the handling qualities of the level fly line are easier for the beginner to adjust to than the use of monofilament.

In any case, behind this 100 foot length of mono or level fly line, the balance of the reel space is taken up by conventional backing line, usually of 20 pound test.

Anytime there's an extensive backpacking-angling trip ahead where there may be a variety of water types calling for a variety of approaches, the shooting taper system is the lightweight, space saving, and versatile way to go.

# Fly Rods

At the mention of backpack fishing, most people visualize one of two general situations. The first is the image of small brushy streams and backwoods ponds. The other is the high ponds and lakes of the western mountain regions. Certainly these are within the scope of the backpacking angler, but there is considerably more latitude than these possibilities. Some judicious searching in virtually any area of the country that offers fair to good trout fishing reveals a wide variety of possibilities for the angler willing to get off the beaten paths. These encompass every conceivable water type and size.

No single rod is always appropriate. In fact I can't think of a single, long term, serious, fly rodding acquaintance who owns only one fly rod. In the normal course of expanding experience, various rods are acquired to best suit variable seasonal or water type requirements. Yet, there should be a reasonably versatile starting point that doesn't compromise too much in the dual requirements of a gentle fly delivery or comfortable handling of the average casting distance requirements. Taken on a nationwide basis, the best selling fly line weight is a number 6, which is a reasonable compromise for the average backpacker. It's enough line weight to cast well and handle a range of fly sizes and types, but it is still light enough to present a fly gently in demanding presentation circumstances. There are any number of fly rods calibrated to swing in phase with a 6 weight line. They vary considerably in material, price, length, and number of rod sections.

Although there are some other possibilities peeking over the horizon, the general availability of materials at this time includes bamboo, boron-graphite blends, graphite, and fiberglass. For average use all of them can be excellent, and all of them can be considerably less than excellent. Material itself is only a starting point of potential. The designed taper establishes the action or feel, and a number of manufacturing variables further influence how well that inherent potential of a material is exploited and translated into user satisfaction. A great deal of the current rod advertising is material oriented. Obviously material is important, but the fact remains that how a material is handled in design, taper, and manufacturing always has been, and will remain, of at least equal importance.

For average use, most rod builders feel a beginning point fly rod should exhibit a smoothly progressive loading ability with the whole rod capable of contributing nicely to the cast. This medium taper should enable the user to handle a short, accurate line nicely, and exhibit the ability to reach well out when a longer line is called for.

That final material choice is elusive and to some extent may be price dependent. In general, bamboo is the most expensive choice, followed by graphite-boron combinations, then graphite, and fiberglass at the lower end of the price range. Each material has its adherents. They all have some appeal for segments of the buying public's taste and preference. For backpacking use, bamboo is the

*Vivian Shohet of The Bamboo Rod, Weston, Vermont, manufactures his Green Mountain Backpacker bamboo rod in two versions: a 7 ft., 4 piece model for lines 4 and 5, and another 7 ft., 4 piece version for lines of 6 and 7 weight. Many offerings of the pack rod concept are available in graphite and glass for packing ease.*

minority material. It is the most expensive and occupies the minor volume segment of the market anyway. Still, some anglers prefer this traditional material to all other alternatives. Graphite has come a long way in a few short years. The early problems of ferrule breakage and overall durability are virtually eliminated. Further, the tapers and actions have improved, and there is a wide choice of rod lengths and a greater availability of three piece long rods that are convenient to pack. Glass has a thirty year technology and design. Despite the "press" that newer materials are receiving, glass is an excellent value that should not be overlooked, especially if price is a consideration.

The length of the rod and the number of sections are as elusive and personal as the choice of material from which the rod is made. I could name several well known anglers with a basic agreement on what line weight is functionally suited to a particular piece of water, but the rod they choose to swing to support that same line weight varies by a full 3 feet—from 6 to 9 feet. To further complicate the matter, each of these anglers could come up with a reasonably plausible explanation to justify their particular choice. The short rod advocate delights in the intimate feel of the little sticks. He believes he has a greater "feel" for the casting, hooking, and playing of the fish. In windy conditions he feels he's able to keep the line low and close to the water. With his stiff, fast-tipped rod he can fire a neat, tight loop, almost under the wind as it were. A long rod advocate counters by pointing out his own sense of control. He can pick a longer line off the water nicely, avoid sagging backcasts into streamside brush, and he can guide the drift of the fly and make any line mending corrections more easily.

Since the go-light guy or gal needs as much versatility as possible, let's look at a couple of other options. In addition to the straightforward concept of the pack rod, there are some combination rods worth consideration: the fly-spin possibility or the spin-fly possibility. Again, it's a matter of limited availability in bamboo with more offerings available in graphite or fiberglass. And there are various ways of handling the concept. If the emphasis is on fly rod function and using a spin reel as an accommodation, the makers start with a standard fly rod blank. Then, the individual approach is varied. Some makers utilize a long, level, cork grip and sliding reel bands which accommodate the fly reel in its conventional rear of the grip location, and permit repositioning in mid-grip for the spin reel. The first one or two guides are sometimes slightly oversized to help funnel down the spiraling spin line.

Each angler has creditable arguments, but I'd have to advise the newcomer to avoid each extreme. Short, light rods are a delight. A quick appraisal of their characteristics, however, indicates that they are better in the hands of the experienced angler, for timing and casting smoothness are more critical if they are to perform at their maximum. The very long rods may be a nuisance in confined quarters even though the arguments of line control and mending ease are still valid. Also, if one is consistently wading deep or working out of a float tube, extra rod length is helpful. Presumably our theoretical backpacking angler will be fishing a variety of waters through the course of a usual season.

*For the one-rod backpacking angler, the combination fly/spin concept is popu-*
*lar. Sliding reel bands permit positioning of the spin reel in mid-grip or*
*mounting the Orvis CFO reel further back in the conventional location.*

Extremes in rod length at either end should be avoided.

In double-checking some preferences for our hypothetical #6 rod, I've consulted a number of anglers and rod building friends. The averages come out about like this: In bamboo, the most popular length is $7\frac{1}{2}$ feet, followed by 8 feet, then 7 feet; in glass, the most popular is an 8 foot model, closely and almost equally followed by $8\frac{1}{2}$ feet and $7\frac{1}{2}$ feet; in graphite, the 8 foot, $8\frac{1}{2}$ foot and 9 foot lengths for a 6 weight line are almost equally popular. There were quite a few who qualified this latter observation by saying that anglers working open rivers and ponds were tending toward the 9 foot for 6 as their first choice.

Most middle range fly rods handle at least a couple of line sizes with reasonable satisfaction. The best rod designs aim at a particular line weight, but because of line weight distribution (double taper versus weight forward and shooting tapers trailed by very light running lines, plus rod taper design and material characteristics) there is quite a bit of versatility inherent in most models. For example, if your rod handles 35 or 40 feet of a double taper 6 without any problem, it's bound to handle one belly size larger in a weight forward (a #7). Since the weight-aware backpacker is in need of versatility, I'd suggest you try your current fly rod with a line size lighter than recommended as well as a line size heavier than recommended, particularly in weight forward and shooting tapers. You may find you're able to customize to some extent to contend with differing circumstances.

The two piece rods are the most popular, and a two piece 8 foot rod isn't at all hard to pack. If you're up into a 9 foot graphite rod, then you might look for a three piece model for extra convenience. Modern ferruling methods can be so good you'll never notice any functional difference in performance, and the transport of the rod is somewhat easier. Some backpackers contend that only a true pack rod of 3 to perhaps 5 pieces is worth consideration because of transport ease. I doubt this is a really valid observation. Probably ninety percent of all the backpacking done by the angler is on trails, and even if rather extensive bushwhacking or off-trail travel is to be done, this is not an automatic assumption that the travel will be tough. Some areas are open and easy to travel. When the going is through tough brush, you'll have your own bulk and that of the pack to contend with. I can't see that the minor addition of a rod case taped alongside the frame will make a great deal of difference in travel ease. In other words, if you don't own a pack rod, just take along whichever rod you own that's capable of doing the job at the destination.

If you do prefer the pack rod concept, there are a number from which to select: a few in bamboo, more still in graphite and fiberglass. As I've hinted at previously, the fact that a rod breaks down into multiple sections should not imply a lessening of performance. You have a right to expect good performance. The quality rod builder can make these multi-sectioned models almost indistinguishable from the more standard two piece models. There's no question they are very convenient to pack.

Another common approach uses a reversible handle, set one way for fly reel use, reversed for spin reel use. This also works. Beyond the fact that the concept exists, how does it perform? Actually, quite well. The fly rod usage should feel normal as the blank is a normal fly rod taper. A fly rod blank set up in this manner is a good light spin option. On the assumption that you'll be using a small spin reel to begin with, with a none too large spool diameter, there is no real problem in funneling the spinning line through the guides. I have one especially hardheaded friend who swears by such a rig. His prejudices include sinking lines, despite any number of lectures. He uses a graphite fly-spin rod with a floating fly line. He lengthens leaders and adds twist ons for some subsurface work, but if the fish are lying deep, he just switches to an ultra-light spin reel. His results are excellent, and perhaps, more importantly, he finds it fun. That is difficult to argue with.

The flip side of the coin is the angler who is primarily a spin fisherman and would like to use a fly occasionally. The starting point is a spin blank set up to accommodate this occasional fly line usage. To illustrate the concept, there is one (of multiple offerings) from Fenwick. Their SF74-4 is a 7 foot pack rod with a recommended spin lure weight range from $\frac{1}{8}$ to $\frac{3}{8}$ ounces, using 2 through 6 pound monofilament. Or, it can carry a #6 fly line instead. The rod weight is $4\frac{3}{4}$ ounces, the pack length is 24 inches and when it's in its carrying case there is a total pack weight of 14 ounces.

If the concept of such versatility is appealing but at present you only own a fly rod or a spin rod, don't despair. Take the fly rod out in the yard with an ultra-light spin reel. You can mount it in the normal fly reel location (but I'd suggest you try taping it to the mid-portion of the cork grip). Try lures from about $\frac{1}{8}$ to $\frac{1}{4}$ ounce in trial casts. Due to the usual taper differences between a fly rod and a standard spin rod, you'll find the casting stroke slower; but, overall the concept can work out fine, and it can bring another possible approach to your go-light travels. In some areas this is a fairly routine practice. Mickey Powell at Buz's Fly and Tackle in Visalia, California has mentioned that several backpackers in the high Sierras are primarily fly roders but they often tuck an ultra-light spin reel in their gear for those moments when the fish are either deep or distant.

The owner of a conventional spin rod can also try for this extra potential. Mount a fly reel in place. If the rod is a fairly typical light model designed for lures in the $\frac{1}{4}$ ounce range, try a weight forward or shooting taper in 6 and 7 fly line weights and see how it works.

The spin angler who has never tried fly casting before still has one more approach that is useful when flies are obviously required. Little gadgets called spin bubbles may save the day. These are clear plastic and can be filled with water, mineral oil, etc. for casting weight. There are a couple of versions of the idea. One is a free-sliding bubble available in two sizes. The smaller one weighs $\frac{1}{4}$ ounce when filled; the larger one weighs $\frac{1}{2}$ ounce when filled. In normal use, slip the spin line through the bubble and tie a perfection loop at the end of the spin line. Above this perfection loop (and below the bubble) place a stop which can be a split shot for subsurface fly use or ust a knot of string for floating fly use. Loop a short leader onto the perfection loop you previously formed at the end of the spin line. Then tie on the appropriate fly at the end of the leader. As you make the cast, check it as the bubble nears the water to turn the leader over and extend the fly. The free-sliding bubble permits you to strike directly through to the fish with no interference from the bubble. It may not be the neatest rig in existence, but it does work and gives the spin angler the option of using flies. This extends versatility and keeps overall gear weight to a minimum.

Although we've emphasized the 6 weight outfit as generally appropriate, it is equally true that exceptions exist. Going slightly lighter or heavier may be more appropriate for your individual requirements. If you have questions, seek out expert local help from anglers and tackle shops. Also, if you want to travel light and be as flexible as possible in your approaches, try some of the experimenting outlined. Try fly lines of differing weights; try a spin reel on your fly rod; or a fly line on your spin rod. If you are a confirmed spin angler, pick up a couple of the spin bubbles and a few flies. No single method is always productive. You'll be better prepared to handle changing situations if you are aware of the various alternatives possible, even when traveling light. Certainly some of these are compromises of a sort but they work and may make the difference between taking fish and going empty-handed. As one fishing friend remarked after I'd chided him on an unorthodox, but successful, approach, "Sometimes it's better to be potent than pure."

# Fly Reels

The fly reel for the backpacker is the standard single action model. As the handle makes one complete revolution, the spool also makes one complete revolution—a direct ratio. In use, the reel stores the line and backing and assists in playing the fish. The angling norm is to make the cast and immediately bring the fly line to the forefinger of the rod hand. Then all retrieves or line manipulations are done behind this rod holding hand. The handling of the line over this rod hand forefinger assures an immediate strike response and control. Any excess slack which may exist at this time is quickly taken onto the reel, and the fish is handled off the reel. A small fish may be summarily stripped in by hand, but all desirable fish require being worked off the reel. Any excess slack line always seems to find a way to tangle, causing the tippet to part and the resultant loss of the fish. Although the fly reel selected should have an adjustable drag, most experienced hands set this at the minimum setting, or just enough so the reel spool doesn't overrun when line is quickly stripped. Then the setting is never varied. The fish can be handled by rod angle counter adjustments. If additional drag is required, palm the reel. The hand provides greater response speed and sensitivity than any mechanical drag.

The usual trout reel varies from about 3 inches to some $3\frac{1}{2}$ inches in diameter, and the weight factors run from a bit under 3 ounces to over 5 ounces.

*The Hardy* LRH Lightweight *is one of the top of the line choices for single-action fly reel selection for any angler.*

Weight is not a functional criterion. Reel makers combine excellent strength and durability from lightweight alloys, aluminum, and other materials. The more immediate consideration is adequate capacity for the intended use, although the weight-conscious backpacker may look to the lighter end of available choices. But, by no means should weight alone be the influencing factor in making the decision. Because single action fly reels are inherently simple, some overlook quality construction features. However, any equipment malfunction or breakdown when you're far removed from an alternative is disastrous, so a quick appraisal of the apparent quality is worthwhile. For instance, the reel frame supports the spool axle and drag parts and, being subject to a great deal of vibration, it is advantageous if the number of screws in the frame construction is kept to a minimum. Further, since the axle is supported only on one side

*The Cortland CG Graphite fly reels are available in three sizes, weigh less than conventional aluminum reels, and feature adjustable drag, spool interchangeability, and easy conversion for right or left hand use.*

where it is attached to the reel frame, it must be firmly attached. The axle itself should have an adequate bearing surface to absorb the continual movement of the spool. The handle should be easy to grip, yet small and probably tapered to blend well and minimize the possibility of slack line tangling on it. A quick spool release permits access for cleaning the reel. If you are using extra spools, this feature makes for rapid and secure interchangeability. The reel foot should also be firmly secured to the frame, again so that it won't vibrate loose after a period of time.

Traditionally fly reels are seated so a right-handed caster has the reel handle on the right and changes hands while playing a fish. More and more anglers seem to be converting to left hand wind so they don't change hands. Although most reels come set up with the handle on the right, they permit easy conversion to left hand wind if the individual desires.

Have the line come to within $\frac{1}{4}$ or $\frac{3}{8}$ of an inch of the cross braces. If it doesn't, then a backing line is in order. The average trout isn't about to make a long sizzling run. However, the backing is otherwise functional in that it provides a larger arbor for the line to be wound over, minimizing any tendency for the fly line to take tight reel coils. It also permits more rapid line recovery and, of course, it is vital insurance for the occasional big trout which may decide to go places beyond the normal fly line length. Presumably many backpackers will set up a shooting taper system anyway which requires a great deal of backing if the reel is to be filled to within the $\frac{3}{8}$ of an inch of the cross braces that we recommend. Guessing at the required capacity is patently impossible. One method of working out this capacity question involves two similar capacity reels or a reel and an extra spool. Say you've got the 30 foot shooting head, the 100 feet of monofilament or level fly line and a bulk spool of 20 pound dacron or micron backing. Wind the front tip of the shooting head onto the empty reel, loop or tie the mono or level fly line, and continue winding until you come to the backing. Then loop or tie the backing and wind until the reel is almost filled (to that $\frac{3}{8}$ of an inch figure we've mentioned), and cut the backing. If you are working with a reel and an extra spool, you may now remove the spool from the reel and have someone hold it for you. Place the new empty spool in the reel and reverse wind it by tying the backing end to the reel and cranking until everything is set in a normal manner. If you have an extra reel, just reverse wind from the one to the other.

Like most choices in angling or backpacking equipment, there is a fair range of prices from which you can choose. The inflationary spirals of recent times have pushed some of the top quality reels high in price, but these products are closely machined to fine tolerances. They are durable and well made in every respect. Some of these top offerings are the fly reels from Hardy, Orvis, and Scientific Anglers. In the medium price ranges there are a larger number of choices. Careful scrutiny locates well-made, durable reels that provide trouble-free reliable service.

# The Leader

The leader is critically important to the fly fisherman's success. A more or less invisible connection from the fly line to the fly, the leader must be flexible enough to permit the fly to respond to subtle current flows so the behavioral characteristics of the artificial fly appear natural and lifelike to the trout. In order for the leader to perform these multiple functions, it is tapered from a relatively large diameter butt section where it joins the fly line down through a diminishing diameter or taper graduation to the final tippet section to which the fly is attached.

Leaders are available in both knotted and knotless styles. Some specialists argue the relative merits of each but we're treading a fundamental path here, and both styles can perform admirably under most conditions as long as they are properly designed.

The usual commercial availability of tapered leaders in both styles is $7\frac{1}{2}$ feet, 9 feet and 12 feet. On very small streams where there is apt to be a minimum of line length beyond the rod tip, and line speed may be less than normal, a short, quick turning taper is handy. The $7\frac{1}{2}$ foot lengths are usually appropriate. An average length is probably the 9 foot model. On the average-sized stream and normal casting lengths of 15 feet to 40 feet, the 9 footer carries well. If the water is very low and clear or the flies are very small, most anglers prefer the longer 12 foot models. One other relationship should be mentioned: the relationship between tippet diameter and fly size. Without a harmonious relationship here, a tiny fly may be as difficult to present properly as a much larger fly offering.

On the average, a specific diameter can support and transmit energy effectively through a range of three hook sizes. Beyond that range, chances are the tippet will require alteration to a heavier or lighter diameter for best performance. Assume you're working along with a 12 foot leader tapered to 6X with a small #20 dry in place. From a casting and presentation standpoint everything is performing well, but there are no rising fish. You decide to tie on a larger attractor type of fly such as a #12 Spider. Suddenly the smoothness is gone, the fly falls back on the leader, the leader tippet twists or it falls to lie alongside the leader rather than straightening out. What has happened is essentially this: The 6X tippet cannot support and transmit enough energy through the larger, more wind-resistant fly pattern now in place. A drastic shortening of the tippet may provide some improvement but the real answer is a larger diameter tippet that effectively supports and turns the fly properly. The following chart is a starting point for average use:

| tippet size | fly size | tippet size | fly size |
|---|---|---|---|
| 0X (.011) | 2 to 1/0 | 5X (.006) | 14,16,18 |
| 1X (.010) | 4,6,8 | 6X (.005) | 16-22 |
| 2X (.009) | 6,8,10 | 7X (.004) | 18-28 |
| 3X (.008) | 10,12,14 | 8X (.003) | 20-28 |
| 4X (.007) | 12,14,16 | | |

Related to this discussion is monofilament "memory" or its tendency to retain tight packaging coils. These should be removed before starting to fish. Most limp materials can be straightened by hand. Pull to stretch them somewhat, then gradually release the tension. Additionally there are commercial aids, leader conditioners of leather or rubber. The tops of your rubber waders are handy for this. If the heavier butt portions haven't straightened satisfactorily by hand, the conditioners are useful. Be sure not to rub too vigorously. Frictional heat is generated and too much heat may damage the molecular structure of the monofilament. The monofilament has a specific gravity somewhat in excess of water. In theory it will sink by itself. However, the tendency is for it to remain buoyed up by normal surface tension. There are a number of commercial leader sinks which some anglers regularly use. Others question or discount the importance of a leader tippet floating or sinking in normal dry fly use and ignore the question entirely. Their continued successes tend to indicate that in most instances a natural, drag free and lifelike behavior of the artificial fly which is achieved through tippet length and flexibility is a more important consideration than whether the tippet floats or sinks. Still, there may be specific instances when a portion of the tippet should be sunk. Lacking a commercial preparation use mud, silt, or aquatic vegetation to "treat" the section. If you want to be sure the leader will float while fishing emergent or floating mayfly nymphs, midge pupae or caddis pupae, treat the leader with any of the silicone based preparations such as *Mucilin* or *Gink*.

Although the 7½, 9 and 12 footers are the commercial norm, there are occasions when longer or shorter leaders can be used. Several pond and lake specialists working with floating lines are going to very long knotted tapers of 20 feet or more. Conversely, anglers using sinking lines have found that deeplying fish are not leader shy. To counteract the natural tendency for the leader to sink very slowly, more slowly than their sinking fly lines, they compensate by shortening their leaders, which may run from about 2 feet to 6 feet in length. These can be as simple as a single strand of monofilament or no more than three pieces of monofilament of different diameters knotted together. The level at which a fly works is vital. These extra short leaders are very effective. From a standpoint of simplicity, there is one more system that is gaining in popularity with some anglers. It consists of making a permanent loop in the end of the leader and looping the desired tippet to it in a loop to loop connection. The looped tippets are prepared beforehand at home and quickly added on the stream. In fact, if you have an idea of what fly you'll want to use as dusk settles, you can prepare totally in advance by knotting on the fly choice to the other end of the looped tippet and minimize the struggles as dusk settles and the activity starts.

The backpacker's needs are often variable with the water types he encounters, so it's probably best to acquire a basic set of tapers in the 7½, 9 and 12 foot lengths as a starting point. Add a few spools of tippet material in the required size ranges, and you'll be able to adjust for whatever conditions are encountered.

# Tackle Selection

As separate activities, both backpacking and fishing are potentially gadget-laden endeavors. When they're combined the situation is even more complex. A careful appraisal of an item's usefulness-to-weight ratio is essential for trips of any length.

In addition to the specifics of tackle item selection is the question of rod case transport. I've seen some backpackers carry the rod case in hand, using it as a walking staff of sorts. However, if both hands are needed to negotiate a tough stretch of terrain, this is a real nuisance. Kelty used to (and may still) offer a better answer in an inexpensive little item they called a fish pole sock. Essentially it looks like a tube sock, $1\frac{3}{4}$ inches in diameter and 6 inches long with a draw string at the top. A rod case of any length can be enclosed. The idea is to tie it to the packframe side member just above a cross bar and let the sock support the weight of the rod. The upper part of the rod case can be secured parallel to the frame side member with a sturdy elastic band, or perhaps better yet, it can be taped in place. As an alternative to the fish pole sock, I've used an old reel bag in the same way, tying it to the frame and taping the upper part of the rod case in place. Something like this can easily be made up at home, and is much easier than trying to carry a rod case in hand.

If the destination is a pond or lake, I add the weight of either a float tube (belly boat) or an inflatable pack raft. There are few things more frustrating than walking several miles to a backcountry pond and finding all the fish working out of reach. The weight and space of either accessory is worthwhile.

*Tony Atwill takes to the water with an inflatable pack raft. Just under 5 lbs. in total weight, the use of such a raft opens up new opportunities for the backpacking angler.*

---

I've had both items for several years and they've always performed admirably. In addition to my pack raft's normal use of moving me from here to there on the water, it's seen some service as a wilderness bathtub, weather shelter, and even a boat bed. I carry some lightweight rope which can be marked heavily at measured intervals with a permanent pen marker, or knotted at intervals to help determine depth. A rock can be tied to the end of the rope to help as a depth probe and anchor of sorts as well. Despite a lot of hard use the raft has stood up extremely well, but I've been concerned about future replacement possibilities, as my American Safety raft has been discontinued. Fortunately Del Canty has come along with an alternative and the only lightweight pack raft that I'm currently aware of. Del is a very skilled specialist who has been taking giant trout for years from float tubes and to a lesser extent from pack rafts. The basic specifications of his pack raft read just about the same as my old American Safety standby, and the use of such a lightweight, portable, and durable pack raft can do wonders for the angling results in many areas.

When I don't take the pack raft, it is the belly boat that goes along. There are "plastic fins" on the market that help propel you around in the float tube, but I prefer swim fins. These can be carried in the pack or lashed outside the pack when walking.

For backcountry river work when wading is required, I use the new Royal Red Ball *Flyweight* stocking foot waders and their felt-soled wading shoes. The waders only weigh only about 12 ounces and are amazingly tough and durable. These have filled a real need for the backcountry angler, and are proving equally popular for normal day to day angling as well.

Beyond these specialized items, the tackle selection is up to the individual. For most trips, not much gear has to be taken. Most tackle will probably all fit in a side pocket of the pack. Generally a fishing vest isn't needed. If one is deemed necessary, the two lightest weight possibilities I'm aware of are the *Warm Weather Tac-L-Pak* from Orvis and the *Furnace Creek Vest* from Tim Boyle at Columbia Sportswear in Portland, Oregon. Each is essentially a bunch of holes held together by nylon with ample pocket capacity for the needs of any packer-angler. Some hikers carry their gear in a small belt bag or fanny pack. Also, an inexpensive day bag may be a handy accessory for splinter day travels out of an established camp site. Normally I just head out with the Orvis *Fishing Shirt*. It's comfortable on the trail, and the large pockets hold all the flies and small accessories I'll need. If more pockets are needed, they can be added at home with a modicum of sewing ability. These added, extra pockets can then be sized and located to suit individual requirements.

A few items may be considered more or less standard for both backpacking and backcountry fishing: a knife, rain jacket, insect repellent, a hat, and polarized sunglasses. The hat and sunglasses are also safety precautions on windy days when working from the pack raft or belly boat—just in case an errant cast swings in too close to you.

Specifically—do you have, want or need:

*pack raft or float tube*
*lightweight stocking foot waders and wading shoes*

*fly rod, spin rod or combination fly-spin rod appropriate to destination water*
*   types and requirements*
*fly reel with extra spool and line or fly reel with a variety of shooting tapers*
*leaders and extra tippet materials*
*plastic or aluminum fly boxes and desired fly types and sizes*
*spin reel with extra spool of heavier or lighter line*
*tape—to secure a spin reel to a fly rod cork grip for special purpose*
*double duty use of the fly rod as a spin rod accommodation*
*spin bubble—for using flies on a spin rod if desired*
*ball bearing snap swivels*
*lure box with variety of spin lures*
*fishing shirt or alternative—vest, belt bag, fanny pack and light day bag*
*folding net—i.e.,* North Fork *pocket net or* Insta-Net *by Handy Pak*
*Flex-Light or similar small, convenient alternative*
*weights—split shot, twist-on lead, lead sleeves or alternatives*
*strike indicator—for subsurface fly work when using floating line methods*
*scissor pliers, folding scissors, or angler's clipper*

| | |
|---|---|
| *leader conditioner* | *rain jacket* |
| *leader sink* | *knife* |
| *line cleaner/dressing* | *hat* |
| *fly floatant* | *polaroids* |
| *stream thermometer* | *insect repellent* |

*hook hone—to touch up dulled hooks*
Dry-Ur-Fly *absorbent powder to restore soaked and matted flies*
*permanent pen markers to alter colors of flies as needed*
*surgical forceps as hook disgorger*
Perhaps a bit more specialized—*aquarium net for picking insects off the water*
*   to determine size, color, etc.; insect collecting vials; stomach pump; magni-*
*fying glass; portable fly tying gear; notebook and pencil;* Arcticreel; *and*
*whistle for emergency use.*

Don't be concerned about the length or complexity of these listings. They serve as an overview of a range of possibilities. The individual should select or modify to suit his or her own needs. Here, for instance, is the go-light approach of one friend for small to medium-sized back country streams in the Northeast. He ties a series of dries in two styles and three sizes. The styles are parachute and a Wingless Hackle pattern that comes out looking like a spider; the sizes are 12, 16 and 20. They're made up in only one light color. He explains that the parachute is low floating, invariably lands upright on the water, and is stable in any water type from slow to fast. The Wingless Hackle patterns have a slightly oversized hackle spread (a #16 would have a normal-sized #14 hackle) to provide a contrasting approach of a higher riding, sparser silhouette. At streamside he alters both types with permanent pen markers to suit the color requirements of the moment. For evening spinner falls he scissors the hackled patterns top and bottom for a reasonable shape approximation. He's adding

*Only about 12 ounces, the Royal Red Ball stocking foot wader system is ideal for the backcountry angler and is proving equally popular for normal day to day angling.*

another "down wing" series of flies for this season to suggest caddis and stone-fly activity.

Some of these flies will be made up on 2X and 3X long shank hooks. When appropriately colored at streamside with pen markers, he figures they will be close enough for cricket and grasshopper activity as well. He does carry a few distinctive shapes, such as ants and beetles, which are otherwise difficult to obtain by alteration. A standard, all purpose nymph like the Gold Ribbed Hare's Ear is tied on standard shank lengths as well as longer shanks. A few are also made up on dry fly hooks for emergent or floating nymph activity. These are also fine tuned as needed with permanent pen markers. For wet flies he relies on a few standards such as a dark Wooly Worm, Picket Pin, Bread-crust, and Brown Hackle Peacock. They supplement his bait fish imitations of Muddler, Grey Ghost, Black Nose Dace and White Marabou.

Some fly floatant, twist-on leads, folding scissors, spare leaders, and tippet material make up the other basic items. If a specific fly is expected to be of particular importance (such as the mid to late season "Trico") he'll make up specific imitations. But overall his frame of mind is to get as much mileage out of a minimum amount of gear as possible. He succeeds surprisingly well. Adding to this success is his experience and careful observation. He pays a great deal of attention to approaching working fish and takes time to maneuver around to a good position or angle from which to deliver his casts accurately and neatly. These down-to-earth requirements are important factors of angling consistency.

# Lure Selection

A quick visit to the nearest, well-stocked tackle shop or an evening spent reading through a few angling catalogs reveals a bewildering array of available spin lures. At the other extreme there are some experienced hands who depend wholly on a specific lure or type of lure. If that singular approach fails them, the fish simply aren't hitting. Nestled somewhere between these extremes there is a functional, common sense starting point. There is a long way between tackle shops in the backcountry, so versatility is the ultimate goal.

The basic types of lures for the spin fisherman are spinners, spoons, jigs, and plugs. A starting selection should be made within this framework.

*SPINNERS:* The little mountain stream sparkled invitingly in the mid-summer sun as we shed our packs and took a break from our sweaty hike. As we sat, sipping the cool water, an angler rounded the downstream bend. We watched as he flipped a little lure about twenty-five feet upstream into a shallow run. He angled the rod far to his right and began retrieving, guiding the lure close to the shadowy side of a large boulder. A chunky little rainbow knifed out to intercept the swim and was soon landed.

A few moments later the angler joined us and noted that this was his fourth fish of the morning. A look at the stream and you'd have thought there wasn't a trout in it. The droughty conditions revealed every pebble, yet tucked away in pools wherever there was a semblance of cover were spunky little trout. The visiting angler had chosen the right weapons for these conditions: a short five foot rod, ultra-light real spooled with two pound mono and a tiny $\frac{1}{16}$th ounce spinner. This stream is typical of many small, mountainous waters in mid-summer: barely moist in the shallows, then dropping off into little runs and pools a foot or so deep.

Conventional $\frac{1}{4}$ ounce spinners or spoons would have been almost impossible to manipulate in the skinny water, their weight demanding a hastier retrieve else they sink artlessly to the bottom. The little lightweight spinner could twinkle along slowly and made all the difference. The angler had also handled the little spinner correctly, first estimating where the fish might lie and casting far enough above the suspected hideaway so he wouldn't alarm the fish. This permitted him to get the lure under control, establish a fishable depth, and steer the lure close to cover. These are sound tactics regardless of the method employed.

In shallow waters spinners are often easier to handle than wobbling spoons, for the revolving blade offers increased resistance, permitting a slow, snag-free retrieve. If choosing between two spinners of equal weight but different blade size, the general rule is that the larger of the two blades offers increased resistance. This allows a slower retrieve which is often better in shallow sections, slow-water sections, and in lakes when fish are cruising near the surface. A narrow-bladed spinner requires more water pressure. Therefore, it fishes deeper and handles better in quick stream runs. Both types have their obvious uses and advantages.

Occasionally the configuration of the stream is such that a downstream cast is needed. If this is the case, the spinners offer excellent lure control. They can be worked back at varying speeds or even held steady. In spite of the sometime advantage in downstream directions, the general rule is to take advantage of the trout's into-the-current posture and work upstream. Closer approaches, enhanced accuracy, and lure control are some of the upstream directed advantages. Tactically, the thinking is the same, whether on an upstream or downstream path. Aim the cast beyond the anticipated lie of the fish and steer the lure to work in close to the suspected hotspot. Swim the lure to the fish at an effective level rather than dropping it in on his head. Attract the fish, don't alarm it.

In large streams thorough water coverage is the prerequisite approach. Try casts angled upstream and just slightly across the current, bringing the lure back at about the same speed as the existing current. Casting cycles should always be progressive in nature, starting close and extending outward in successive casts. When the upstream areas within easy reach are covered, try casting across and just slightly upstream and allow the lure to work around in semicircular sweeps. Enlarge on this concept with successive casts progressively covering a bit more water. When all the reachable water has been thoroughly covered, move and start again with the progressive short, medium, long casting coverages. You should, of course, always be alert for any singular fish holding possibilities which may exist along current edges: drop offs from shallow to deeper waters, along fallen logs, by bouldery obstructions, near undercut banks, and the like.

In the little streams the $\frac{1}{16}$th ounce spinners are about ideal and there would be a bit of leeway for both slightly lighter and slightly heavier lures. In larger rivers the lures can be scaled up and the 3/16th to $\frac{1}{4}$ ounce sizes are apt to be more suitable.

A basic selection of spinners should include a variety of finishes or color combinations. Try to select something with dull or dark tones, then something with medium tones, and finally choose something with light or bright tones. This enables you to suit a lure to specific water clarity conditions.

*SPOONS:* Spoons are among the most popular of the various spin lures for the fundamental reason that they are very effective. Their selection can be related in part to water conditions, depths to be fished, and perhaps even the time of year. Our twin activities of backpacking and angling are primarily three-season sports. Early in the season, when the ice has recently left the ponds and lakes, the water temperature is about the same from top to bottom. Trout tend to work the shallow waters actively at this time. In many areas, such as the northeastern lakes, there may be smelt runs into various tributary streams. We can expect trout and landlocked salmon to forage aggressively through such schooling fish. A wobbling spoon that will fish high in the water is an excellent choice. When selecting between two spoons of equal weight but different blade size, we can expect the larger blade to sink more slowly and handle higher in the water. This characteristic is the ideal for our early season pond and lake activity, and perhaps again late in the fall when cooler waters prevail and the trout are prowling the shallows with some consistency.

The spoons with the smaller surface area for equal weight do cast more easily against strong winds, tend to work deeper, and sink more rapidly. These characteristics are suited to summer conditions when the depths of various ponds and lakes must be plumbed. Also, in the large, swift streams, the denser spoons are ideal.

The standard large stream starting point is to angle the cast up and somewhat across stream, bringing the wobbler back at about the same speed as the current flow and working it deep. Then you may work into a sweeping semicircular coverage. Cast across stream and just slightly upriver, let the wobbler flutter down and angle around. Enlarge on this concept with slightly larger, progressive, casting arcs.

In the small intimate waters, stick to lightweight spoons around the $\frac{1}{16}$th ounce size. For the larger rivers the one quarter ounce size is again the standard starting point.

There are several lure finishes: gold, brass, copper, silver, black, pearl or

160

abalone and, of course, all the color combinations from red and white through the current craze for natural "fish scale" types. As a starting point I believe it's safest to consider overall tonal values and pick something dull or dark, then a medium tonal value, and finally something light or bright. A final check with a tackle dealer in the general area of your trip can suggest any specific local favorites.

*PLUGS:* Although they are usually associated with heavier bait casting gear and fish other than trout, there are enough mini-plugs available today to demand the attention of the well-rounded spin tackle fan.

Plugs are essentially best suited to the larger streams and ponds. If your backcountry parameters will include these water types, a few plugs are a worthwhile addition to your kit. One advantage of the backpacking angler is that he can set up camp near a stream or pond and not worry about being back for some arbitrary deadline. Large brown trout are notorious night feeders through much of the season, and in the heat of midsummer we can expect an activity burst near dawn. The small surface disturbing plugs provide exceptional results under such conditions. They should be fished very slowly, gurgling and pausing in suggestion of wounded or crippled prey. The various shallow, running and small-jointed plugs also do well under these conditions. On the large streams pay particular attention to the shallow runs ahead of the main pools, then work slowly through the pool to the tailing shallows. Large brown trout do much foraging after dark and they can often be found in surprisingly shallow water seeking small crayfish, minnows and other food forms.

The spring, as streams begin to clear but are still running a bit too cold for good insect activity, is another time when plug-handling anglers score well on large rainbows and browns. During the day they often take up feeding stations beneath and beside fairly heavy main current tongues. The minnow-suggestive plugs do a good job. One angling acquaintance swears by the smaller Rapalas and countdown Rapalas for this time period. His catches are impressive.

*JIGS:* Of all the lures common to the average spin angler's arsenal the jigs are the most overlooked, yet, they have uncommon significance by providing an approach impossible to duplicate with spinners, spoons or plugs. On the broad assumption that these other lures suggestively resemble baitfish and have inherently different action in the water, the common bond between them is that they are usually kept on the move. I know they can take fish when held stationary downstream but most strikes do occur when they are on the move.

Now, consider the jig. It has been used most often in a vertical path. That is, it may be cast from a boat. When it hits bottom it is moved up and down, eventually brought back to the surface and recast. Experienced bonefishermen on southern flats have been using jigs in essentially a horizontal travel with great success. The jig can also be inhaled while sitting stationary. Every trout stream has deep holes or undercut banks where large trout dominate. When the fish are not out in a feeding posture, a lure must travel deep to be seen by these cave dwellers. Deep running wobblers and plugs sometimes draw these fish out, but many of these lazy, domineering fish are reluctant to swing out to a rapidly moving lure. The bottom knocking jig is an approach of singular value. It can be cast, allowed to sink to the bottom and then moved slowly or brought along in bouncing hippity-hopping motions. This is because of the weight distribution of the jig, with its hook at the top and its nose-first sinking action. The jigs may resemble some sculpin, large nymphs, or crayfish. In this regard I'm reminded of a call a few years ago from one of the nation's leading anglers, discussing the possibility of a fall trip to Montana. During the conversation we somehow got on the subject of unusual applications of various flies and lures. He mentioned that the Wiggle Jig, a bonefish lure, had long been a secret weapon for large trout. He was convinced that the stop and go manipulations possible with the Wiggle Jig suggested a small crayfish.

The initial presentations are up and across stream, allowing the jig to work deep and pumping the rod tip to slowly bounce the jig along in erratic, tantalizing hippity-hops. In large streams the jig can work out in a cross-stream move; then let it swing around to a position directly below you. Pump the rod and lower the rod tip to allow the lure to settle on the bottom. Tease it along in a pause and pull motion. Pay particular attention to the open sides of log jams, undercut banks and other deep cover that may harbor a good fish.

The jigs are also effective in ponds and lakes. They work deep in weed bed channels, along drop off edges and other potential spots. At night try the shallows when the large fish move in close under the cover of darkness.

For the average small streams the $1/16$th ounce size is again a good starting point, scaling upwards for the larger, deeper rivers. The first few color choices might be green, brown, and black.

A final consideration that is most important with the single-hooked jigs is to keep them sharp. They are the one lure that may be scooped off the bottom when sitting stationary, so penetration is essential.

# 19.

# REGIONAL RECOMMENDATIONS

## Tips from the Local Experts

Any trout producing area of the country offers great potential for the opportunistic, free-to-go-anywhere angler willing to investigate. Trips can be tailered to seasonal availability and angling interest. Small backcountry streams or ponds, or large rivers or high altitude lakes are all within the scope of the hiker. With some judicious planning there may be the further bonus of angling for very large trout. The consistent taking of large fish is a specialty. It is sound, practical angling requiring skill, patience, and knowledge. Perhaps there's no one quite so qualified to discuss taking large trout consistently as Del Canty. He's devoted years of study and practical application to the development of a "system." In addition to his angling skills, Del is a thoroughly experienced backpacker. He has a small booklet (published by Del Canty's Lunker Hunter Systems, Inc., Leadville, Colorado) highlighting his methods. With his permission we've culled a few observations. For large lakes and floatable rivers he uses either the float tube or the backpacker boat, although his preference is the float tube. With this qualification in mind, here is a part of his comment on basic lake fishing methods.

## From Del Canty

*"The best method is to parallel the shoreline and make casts toward the bank. I usually start out in the afternoon and just wander along, casting every few feet. I don't try to cast very far because it becomes very tiring. However, if I see the movement of what I think is a large fish, I'll make a long cast to him while*

*I think I know where he is. It doesn't pay to wait 'til you get to the fish before casting. Blind casts are not nearly as effective as casting at a target. Early in the evening, I place my line of travel in about 20 feet of water. This way I can usually reach the 10 foot level, and if I cast out, the 30 foot level. On dark days it is better to be on a line of travel over about 10 or 12 feet of water and to cast into about 5 or 6 feet of water. On bright days you may want to be over the 30 foot level so you can reach the 20 and 40 foot depths. Lakes vary as to drop-off depths, so adjust accordingly. One rule of thumb is to use dark flies on light days, and light flies on dark days. In the daytime I usually use a sinking line and at night I use a floating line and a floating or nearly floating fly. I also move into shallower water at night."*

About fishing rivers—*"Large rivers are fished differently from small. This deals with rivers that are floatable. I usually have all my gear aboard either the Boat or Float and watch ahead for spots where I can either come ashore or hold my position by paddling. Occasionally I find places where I can anchor and hit good water.*

*You must learn what is prime water and what is not. Some of the best spots are: at the base of a riffle where fast waters enter slow water; where a coarse gravel bar with open gravel exists to provide good cover for insect brood stock; watch for the deep hole with boulders to provide cover; pocket water with scattered large boulders is also good; big logs will also provide cover; undercut banks are excellent; log jams are also very good; weed beds exist in some slow rivers and provide good cover. Always remember that both the fish and their food require cover. Train yourself to look for cover and your fishing will drastically improve.*

*A floating line is proper where the river is not deep. The sinking line is proper where deep holes are fished or in large deep rivers. Casting to your spots is a good basic technique and works well in most cases. This means casting at angles upstream and down. Sometimes feeding a long line into cover from above will take the wise old fish, so keep it in mind. The real trick is to get yourself into the right position for presentation without making the fish aware of your presence.*

*Small rivers where you can or must wade are best fished with a long nymphing rod and the short line method. Two techniques work well. You can either wade up the stream or stay out of the stream and hit prime spots. In either case, you do not actually cast. Your line is almost always straight down from the rod tip so you can effectively bump your nymph along the bottom lifting it about three inches off the bottom for each bump. When a fish touches your nymph you know it right away.*

*On all rivers, large and small, a study of the available food will tell you what flies and lures to use. Turn over rocks, gather vegetation to see what is hiding there. Always remember, though, the Lunker will be found feeding on large enough fare to sustain his weight."*

There is, of course, considerably more in the Del Canty booklet, but even this

*Del Canty's Fly Recommendations for Wind River area, Bridger Wilderness:*

1. *Copepod*
2. *Grey Nymph*
3. *Grizzly Shrimp*
4. *Wooly Worm—orange body*
5. *Wooly Worm—fluorescent hackle*
6. *Badger Muddler*
7. *Rabbit Minnow*
8. *Moth*

cursory overview helps to indicate the thought process, attention to detail, and purposeful curiosity of the specialist. These are qualities which all anglers are advised to cultivate.

In addition to these qualities, some local knowledge is always advantageous. A number of fine anglers have very kindly offered basic recommendations for regions with which they are particularly familiar.

# MARYLAND THROUGH NORTH CAROLINA MOUNTAINS

## From Lefty Kreh

*Tackle needed for the streams in the mountains of Maryland south through western North Carolina is fortunately simple.*

*So far as ultra-light spinning gear is concerned, about all you require is a* reel carrying 4 pound test line. Two lures will do the trick in every stream, and actually one will work in 90 percent or more of the situations.

I'd suggest using a #0 gold Mepps spinner. It does not have to have any squirrel tail or other adornments. In small streams I let it wash down into the heads of pools from above, allowing the current to spin the blade, while I try to keep the lure near the bottom.

In larger pools I toss the lure up and across stream, so that the blade doesn't turn too fast when you bring it back. Silver Mepps will do the job, but in these clear waters the gold finish seems to be more effective.

I also carry the two-inch gold Rapala floating lure. Be sure it's the floating style. You can fish this by throwing down and across the stream and reeling back in an erratic manner, and you can also toss it into the upper portion of a calm pool and then bring it back by twitching it on the surface, rarely letting it go under. This represents a live, struggling minnow, which few trout can resist.

As for flies, a basic and simple selection will do here, too. If you use the Adams in sizes 12, 16, and 18 (smaller flies are more effective after mid-June), then you'll take fish that are rising to gray or dark-colored insects. And, if you cast the Light Cahill in the same sizes, the trout will respond if they are working over lighter-colored insects. Generally speaking, the Adams will work better early in the season, and the Cahill after mid-June. Along about the end of May there are hatches in incredible numbers of light green inchworms. At this time an imitation is deadly.

As for wet flies, the Lead Wing Coachman and the Hare's Ear are two flies local trouters won't be without.

For nymphs, Poul Jorgensen's light brown, medium and dark brown nymphs, which are tied from fur and really resemble all nymphs, but none in particular are deadly. Most nymphs should be no larger than size 10, and many times those tied on 14 and 16 hooks are better.

The White and Black Marabou are standard early spring streamers. Later, say by June, the smaller imitative streamers, such as the Black Nose Dace and the Spruce Fly are effective. In a summary sentence—you don't need a lot of lure or flies, just a wise selection.

# ADIRONDACKS

## From Lionel Atwill

*DRY FLIES*

Ausable Wulff
Henryville Special
Adams
Blue Wing Olive
Grey Fox

*WET FLIES*

Royal Coachman
Montreal
March Brown

*SPINNING LURES*

Red/White Daredevle
Yellow Jig
Mepps Black Fury
Panther Martin

*NYMPHS*

Green Drake
Zug Bug
Hare's Ear
Dark Stonefly

*STREAMERS*

Muddler Minnow
Black Matuka
Grey Ghost

---

# VERMONT

## From John Merwin

*DRY FLIES: #14 Adams, #20 Black Midge, #14 Woodchuck Caddis*
*WET FLIES: #14 Gold-Ribbed Hare's Ear, #14 Royal Coachman, #14 Black*
*Ant*
*NYMPHS: #14 Tan Caddis Pupa, #14 Hendrickson, #8 Hexagenia Wiggle-*
*Nymph*
*STREAMERS: #6 Muddler, #6 Mickey Finn, #6 Badger Matuka*
*SPINNING LURES:*

*3" Floating Rapala, silver with black back*
*Silver or Gold Flatfish; any of so-called fly-rod sizes*
*Mepps spinner, $1/8$-oz., silver or gold*
*Pheobe Spoon, $1/8$-oz., gold*

# NEW HAMPSHIRE

## From Dick Surette

## SPRING

April—May

| Streamers | | Wet Flies | |
|---|---|---|---|
| Mickey Finn | 6—10 | Black Gnat | 10—12 |
| Grey Ghost | 6—10 | Blue Dun | 10—12 |
| Nine Three | 6—10 | Brown Hackle | 10—12 |
| Supervisor | 6—10 | Hornberg | 6—10 |
| Black Ghost | 6—10 | Montreal | 10—12 |

| Dry Flies | | Nymphs | |
|---|---|---|---|
| Black Gnat | 12—14 | Black Nymph | 12—12 |
| Black Midge | 20—28 | Montana | 6—10 |
| Quill Gordon | 12—14 | Black Sparrow | 8—12 |
| Royal Wulff | 10—12 | Golden Stonefly | 6 |

## EARLY SUMMER

June 1—July 15

| Streamers | | Wet Flies | |
|---|---|---|---|
| Grey Ghost | 8—10 | Quill Gordon | 10—12 |
| Matuka | 8—12 | Hare's Ear | 10—12 |
| Harris Special | 6—10 | Dk. Hendrikson | 10—12 |
| Golden Demon | 6—10 | Hornberg | 10—14 |
| Black Ghost | 6—10 | Muddler | 8—12 |

| Dry Flies | | Nymphs | |
|---|---|---|---|
| Adams | 12—14 | Zug Bug | 10—12 |
| Red Quill | 12—14 | Hare's Ear | 8—14 |
| Grey Fox Variant | 12—16 | Olive Green Caddis | 10—12 |
| Henryville Special | 12—16 | March Brown | 12—14 |
| Cream Caddis | 12—14 | Brown Nymph | 12—16 |
| Hendrikson | 12—16 | | |

# LATE SUMMER

## July 15—Sept. 1

| **Streamers** | | **Wet Flies** | |
|---|---|---|---|
| *Black Nose Dace* | *8—12* | *Professor* | *10—12* |
| *Llama* | *8—12* | *Lt. Cahill* | *10—12* |
| *Maynard Marvel* | *8—12* | *Hornberg* | *12—16* |
| *Little Brook Trout* | *6—10* | *Muddler* | *12—14* |
| *Ballou Special* | *6—10* | *Gray Hackle* | *10—12* |

| **Dry Flies** | | **Nymphs** | |
|---|---|---|---|
| *Grasshopper* | *10—14* | *Atherton Light* | *14* |
| *Spiders* | *14* | *Hare's Ear* | *12—16* |
| *Adams* | *14—18* | *Caddis Pupa* | *10—12* |
| *Ginger Bivisible* | *12—14* | *Midge Pupa* | *18—20* |
| *Blue Wing Olive* | *16—18* | | |
| *Cream Midge* | *20* | | |
| *Black Beetle* | *18* | | |

# FALL

## Sept. 1—Oct. 15

| **Streamers** | | **Wet Flies** | |
|---|---|---|---|
| *Dk. Edson Tiger* | *6—14* | *Muddler* | *6—10* |
| *Lt. Edson Toger* | *6—14* | *Hornberg* | *6—10* |
| *Royal Coachman* | *8—12* | *Royal Coachman* | *10—12* |
| *Warden's Worry* | *6—10* | *Black Gnat* | *14—16* |
| *Mickey Finn* | *10—12* | *Gray Hackle* | *10—12* |

| **Dry Flies** | | **Nymphs** | |
|---|---|---|---|
| *Grasshopper* | *8—12* | *Casual Dress* | *8* |
| *Royal Wulff* | *10—12* | *Hare's Ear* | *8—12* |
| *Black Ant* | *14—20* | *Crayfish* | *6—10* |
| *Bucktail Caddis* | *8—12* | *Olive Nymph* | *12—16* |
| *Blue Dun Midge* | *20* | | |

# MAINE

## From Bob Leeman

When I'm wading or canoeing the central and eastern regions of Maine for Brook Trout, I'm sure to include in my flybox the following selections of flies:

Muddler minnows in sizes ranging from #12 to #8. The muddlers work especially well if there's a slight rise in water, or if it's the least bit turgid.

Grasshoppers: preferably yellow, but some orange. The size #8 hoppers seem to lure the biggest trout to strike.

Buckbugs in sizes 10 and 12. Here's a relatively new fly to us from Canadian waters. I don't really know what the Brookies think it is, but they're intent on destroying it. And, they'll take it fished both wet and dry.

Cahills #12 and #14 in both light and dark shades and Slim Jims in the same sizes are my preferred dry flies.

Parmacheene Belle #14 dries are best on a real bright day on crystalline waters.

Hornbergs and Humpys in size 10 are excellent for both Brookies and Brown Trout. Slightly larger sizes are good for landlocked salmon while casting rivers that have them. The Browns seem to have a passion for yellow colors, so I carry some Yellow Hornbergs especially for them.

I've taken some heavy Landlocked Salmon and trout too, on #12 Picket Pins that come under the category of nymph-wet type flies.

The Green Caddis Latex nymph is always in my flybox during the early part of the season. A Hare's Ear nymph is good, too. Both are weighted.

Professors and Royal Coachmans in sizes #10 and #12 are preferred wet fly patterns. Mosquitoes in small sizes tied real sparse in both wet and dry patterns will often produce when all else fails with finicky trout.

My best casting streamer fly patterns in bigger waters include: Grey Ghost, Pink Lady, Maribou Muddler, and Red and White Bucktail. Best sizes in these are #8 and #10. I try not to forget a Barnes Special for any interested Browns.

There's also the exception to the basic rules. For those occasions which fishermen cannot explain, I always include (and often try) a big #8 White Wulff dryfly and a #8 brown and orange stonefly dryfly.

During late season, low-water September fishing, sizes #18 to #24 Midge dryflies have often saved the day for action. Brown, Black, and Blue Dun patterns are best.

When my ultra-light spinning outfit goes along for both river and pond casting, I make sure I have the following lures with me: Dardevle Midgets in red and white and yellow five-of-diamonds, Al's Goldfish in gold, and a few small, assorted Mepps Spinners in both silver and gold. With this arsenal, I consider myself well prepared. And, everything is light, compact, and easily portaged.

# MIDWEST

## From Dick Pobst

*For the Great Lakes area, we have several different types of fishing to consider. All are with flies and all are in rivers or streams.*

*In spring we start with the steelhead, usually in late March or early April. Typical fly selections include the Spring Nymph, as the most popular, and some of the western patterns such as Skunk, Umpqua, and Skykomish, all on size 4 hooks. However, we have recently found that the steelhead are highly selective to the stonefly nymphs that are active in the water; so now my first choices are a large black stonefly nymph, size 2, and the early black, size 8. Last spring we found that on some days we would get strikes on more than half our casts with the stoneflies.*

*The streamer fisherman would usually be well served with a selection of Muddlers, Matukas, and Black-Nosed Daces.*

*After trout opening day, the last Saturday in April, the early trout fisherman wants to pay special attention to the Midwestern super-hatch chart from Selective Trout. He should have: Hendricksons, size 14; Sulfur Duns, #16; Blue-Winged Olives, #18. In addition, there is a very prolific little Black Caddis, size 16. The Gray Drake, #12, is important on some rivers.*

*For the mid-season, the major hatches are the Brown Drake, #10, and the giant Michigan Mayfly, #6, which hatches after dark. Besides those, it is good to have some #14 light Cahills and #14 and #16 Adams. In case you happen to run into an important caddis hatch, we'd suggest #18 Henryvilles and #16 Kings River patterns. This season is from about the first of June to the 10th of July.*

*For the late trout season, you have: Slate-winged Olives, size 14; White-Winged Blacks, #26; and tiny Blue-Winged Olives, #24. It is also important to have some terrestrials, such as hoppers and ants. Night fisherman use big flies, such as mouse and frog patterns that are used on bass, or big streamers.*

*Sometime in September, the Chinook and Coho Salmon start to move into the rivers. At first they can be taken by fishing big streamers deep in the heads of pools at dusk. By big streamers I mean ones with an overall length of 4 to 6 inches. However, our rivers are short, and once the spawning urge takes hold, the fish move directly from the lake to the spawning redds. We then fish to spotted fish, concentrating on the big dominant males, which run from 25 to 40 pounds, and are very tough. For those we use two-egg sperm flies and salmon muddlers, as well as the steelhead flies, usually on #4 hooks.*

*For spinning, the most popular lures are Mepps spinners fished upstream on ultralight tackle, and there are some very creative fishermen with Rapalas. Quite a few spin with nymphs and split shot.*

*The Keel Flies that are most popular are the Muddler and Black-Nosed Dace*

171

*for fishing some of the loggy, brushy streams (streamer flies).*

*The Keel Dry flies have gained greatest acceptance in the U.S. for fishing the giant mayfly hatch, since it is so easy to get hung up when fishing after dark. Interestingly, the Keel dries have made major impact on the chalk streams of England, due to the interest of Dermot Wilson. John Goddard plans to feature them in a forthcoming book on chalk stream fishing. The reason is that they ride with the hook out of the water, and have the natural curved body of the mayfly.*

*The other Keel flies that have done very well are the floating bass bugs, called Miracle Bugs by Al McClane, and the saltwater patterns.*

---

# COLORADO

## From Charlie Loughridge

*DRIES—(in the high country). #16—18 Royal Wulff, #18—20 Mosquito, #18—20 Black Gnat, #18—20 Light Cahill, #16—18 Grey Parachute (these with a very short deer hair tail, white kip tail wing and brown hackle), #8—10 Grasshoppers, #12—16 Caddis, such as elk hair caddis.*

*WET—Black Wooly Worms #8—10 (without tinsel ribbing, use either brown or grizzly hackle).*

*Other General Recommendations for Colorado Waters: Dry—Adams in #14 and smaller, #12 Royal Wulff and smaller, #20 and 22 Grey Herl Midges. Wets: Grey Hackle Yellow #12, #12 Cowdung. Nymphs: #12—16 weighted, Gold Ribbed Hare's Ear, Muskrat, Renegade and dark stoneflies in #10 through 16. For general spinning, the smaller sizes Mepps spinners in both gold and silver work well.*

---

# WYOMING

## From Del Canty

*My favorite flies for Wind River Area, Bridger Wilderness:*

*Copepod—for the lakes that contain Goldens and other waters that are ideal habitat for Goldens. This means those lakes above 9,500 ft. that have large populations of Copepods. The real thing is about $^1/_{32}$ to $^1/_{16}$ of an inch long, occasionally up to $^1/_8$ inch. The fly is obviously oversize, but it works so don't* *tell the fish, please.*

*Grey Nymph—Represents the Burrowing May, several Caddis and the Grey Midges. It's a good all-around nymph and easy to tie.*

*Grizzly Shrimp—Good wherever Gammarus Scuds exist. That will be wherever the fish are exceptionally plump. The fly is oversize, but again, don't tell the fish!*

*Wooly Worm—Orange Body is for spawning fish.*

*Wooly Worm—Fluorescent hackle for murky water. Fished deep and down the bank, best from float or boat.*

*Badger Muddler—Wherever minnows exist.*

*Rabbit Minnow—Wherever minnows exist.*

*Moth—For moths, evening fishing with floating line.*

*When backpacking, I use the* Fishing Float, Bivouac Bag Inflator, *light swim fins, lightweight waders and* Air Pillow *whenever the per day distance is less than 8 miles. The total weight of this outfit is heavier and also limits me to only about a 5 days' supply of food. I don't like my pack to go over 40 pounds.*

*If I'm on a long trail, (8 to 20 miles per day) I use the* Backpacker's Boat *and paddles,* Bivouac Bag Inflator, *lightweight waders and* Air Pillow. *This weighs about 6$^{1}/_{2}$ pounds and eliminates the need for a tent entirely. I can make it for 2 weeks or more with this lightweight set up. The Fishing Float is the better fishing rig, but lightweight counts too.*

*The way to use either unit is to cast to the shoreline and retrieve down the bank. Sinking line in bright daylight hours, floating line at darker times. Nymphs and minnow imitations for bright sunlight, floating moth and minnow imitations at darker times.*

*The anchor set up helps if its windy. Anchor and fish the rough shoreline, casting with the wind. The fish will come to you; so you don't have to move. My special reel is ideal because of the long casts possible: 100 to 200 feet are reachable with the wind and no tangles.*

---

# PACIFIC NORTHWEST

## From Jim Green and Wray Lertora

*As far as spinning lures are concerned, there are a good many that are popular, but I've found that $^{1}/_{16}$ and $^{1}/_{8}$ ounce gray, brown, black and white Rooster Tails work very well for trout. No. "0" and "1" Mepps Aglia spinners are also very effective. Fishing with small spoons in larger streams and lakes is also very productive. My favorite spoons for this type of fishing are the S-1 Hopkins, the $^{1}/_{8}$ ounce Kastmaster, and $^{1}/_{4}$ Lil Structure Spoon from Saddleback Tackle.*

*Jim has several favorite trout fly patterns for the Northwest. Dry flies include the Renegade, Salmon Candy and the McKenzie Stone.*

*Some productive wet flies and nymphs are the Carey Special, Dragon Fly Nymph, Hutchinson's Damselfly Nymph and the TDC Nymph. The White Marabou Muddler and the Standard Muddler Minnow, Candlelite, and the Skykomish Sunrise are 'favorite' streamers.*

---

# IDAHO

## From Bill Mason

### FLIES

| | |
|---|---|
| *Adams* | *#14—20* |
| *Speckled Spinner* | *#16* |
| *Gray Nymph* | *#14* |

*Adams in larger size, as well as the Speckled Spinner, will imitate the Calibeatis genus of mayflies that far and above is predominate in lakes. The smaller Adams can imitate surface midge activity. Gray Nymph will imitate Calibeatis Nymph.*

| | |
|---|---|
| *Gray Midge Pupa* | *#16—18* |
| *Black Midge Pupa* | *#16—18* |
| *Hemingway Caddis* | *#12—18* |
| *(Henryville type)* | |
| *Mason Brown Caddis Pupa* | *#12—16* |
| *Mason Olive Caddis Pupa* | *#12—16* |
| *Olive Damsel Nymph* | *#10* |
| *Brown Damsel Nymph* | *#10* |
| *Olive Troth Shrimp* | *#12—16* |
| *Otter Shrimp* | *#10—16* |

### LURES

| | |
|---|---|
| *Gold and silver Mepps* | *$^1/_8$—$^1/_4$ oz.* |
| *Panther Martins* | *$^1/_4$ oz.* |
| *Daredevils* | *$^3/_8$ oz.* |
| *Eddie Pope's Hotshot* | *$^3/_8$ oz.* |

# WEST YELLOWSTONE

## From Bud Lilly

*NYMPHS*

*Otter Nymph: weighted #10, 12, 14*
*Black Wooly Worm: 8, 10, 12*
*Olive Wooly Worm: long shank #6, 8, 10*
*Zug Bug: #8, 10, 12*

*STREAMERS*

*Muddler Minnow: weighted #4, 6, 8*
*Light Spruce: #4, 6, 8*
*Hornberg Special: 8, 10*

*WET FLIED*

*Gray Hackle Peacock: #12*
*Lady Mith: #10*
*Ginger Quill: #12*

*DRY FLIES*

*Adams: #14, 16*
*Black Gnat: #16, 18*
*Goofus Bug: #14, 16, 18*
*Grasshopper: #10, 12, 14*
*Pheasant Caddis: #12, 14*
*Blue Dun: #16, 18*

*SPINNING LURES: Mepps #1 and 2 Gold; Jake's Spin-a-lure Gold; Thomas Cyclone Gold, $1/_4$ ounce; Thomas Cyclone Copper, $1/_4$ ounce; Kastmaster gold, $1/_4$ or $3/_8$ ounce.*

---

# WEST COAST

## From Rex Gerlach

*In the Pacific Northwest area, backpacking is done at moderate elevations up to say, around 3700 feet, as well as in the higher elevations. In parts of Washington's Columbia basin, it is done at low elevation down through sand* dune country; so in that area you really have quite a range of flies that may be needed, all the way from effective dragon and damselfly nymph patterns for low elevation seepage lakes, on up through a wide range of mayfly and chironomid imitators used at higher elevations. My recommendation to a backpacker in the Pacific Northwest and in California would be a very well-rounded fly box, including dry flies and nymphs. To imitate mayflies, midges, fresh-water shrimps, damselfly nymphs, dragonfly nymphs, the Ogara Shrimp is one of the better shrimp imitators that I've tried. You'll find that dressing in Sid Gordon's book, How to Fish from Top to Bottom. It's all muskrat-dubbed fur held together with gold wire.

Virtually every Pacific angler has his own dragonfly nymph imitators; most of them work quite well. A good generic pattern that works when both dragonfly and damselfly nymphs are active, is a simple shaped body of olive-colored chenille and a short collar of greenish-brown pheasant rump tied with a single feather. This is usually tied on a 3 to 4× long 8 through 4 sized hooks.

The Royal Coachman Bucktail is a staple at virtually all elevations throughout the Western region from Montana west to Washington down Oregon and California. It's used all the way from size 4 down to size 18—very effective. Any western backpacker should have a few Black Drake Mayfly imitators, size 14, as well as some cream-colored mayflies, ranging down as small as size 22. A small grey sedge in size 22 to 28 is also used.

Insofar as spinning lures go, any good popular lure in the $1/32$ to $1/4$ ounce weight range is effective. I like the little, tiny Mepps and the Panther Martins, as well as any.

---

# SIERRAS

### From Doug McKinsey

DRY FLIES: Adams sizes 12-18; Humpy Yellow sizes 10-16; Calif. Mosquito sizes 12-16; Light Cahill sizes 12-18; Elk Hair Caddis (Troth Caddis) sizes 10-18; Royal Wulff 8-14;
WET FLIES: Western Coachman, sizes 10-14; Timberline Emerger sizes 12-16.
NYMPHS: Gold Ribbed Hairs Ear, sizes 10-14; Black A.P. Nymph sizes 10-16; Golden Stonefly sizes 8-12; Brown Stonefly sizes 4-10 (popular stonefly nymphs like the Whitlock series)
STREAMERS: Muddler Minnow sizes 6-12; Whitlock Sculpin sizes 1-8; Marabou Muddler sizes 6-12; Little Brown Trout sizes 6-10; Little Rainbow Trout sizes 6-10.

---

# REGIONAL CONTRIBUTORS

Lefty Kreh is the author of *Fly Casting with Lefty Kreh, Fly Fishing in Salt Water* and co-author with Mark Sosin of *Practical Fishing Knots.* Skilled in all facets of angling, he is very familiar with the mountain regions of the Southeast.

Bob Leeman writes, hosts a television show, and operates a tackle shop in his native state of Maine.

Dick Surette formerly operated a tackle shop in New Hampshire and is currently Editor-Publisher of the specialty magazine *Fly Tyer.*

Lionel Atwill is a near neighbor in Dorset, Vermont. He formerly edited *Adirondack Life* and has been a contributing editor of *Backpacker* magazine. Currently he is Eastern Field Editor of *Outdoor Life.*

John Merwin is another near neighbor and former managing editor of *Fly Fisherman* magazine. Presently he is Editor-Publisher of *Rod and Reel* magazine. He recently edited the valuable book *Stillwater Trout* (Doubleday) which is a "must read" compilation of information and technique for the increasingly popular quest for trout in ponds and lakes.

Dick Pobst is an innovative angler and author of *Fish The Impossible Places*, the treatise on the Keel Fly concept. He operates a tackle shop in Ada, Michigan.

Charles Loughridge is a skilled angler who helped introduce me to several Colorado waters. He's fished, guided, and operated a tackle shop in Colorado until his recent move to St. Anthony, Idaho.

Del Canty has specialized in angling for large trout from his home base in Leadville, Colorado. He's also spent portions of each season backpacking and fishing in the Wind River areas.

Bill Mason is a skilled and knowledgeable Idaho angler involved with a variety of programs of interest to the angler-packer from his Sun Valley base of operations.

Bud Lilly has fished, guided, and operated a tackle shop for several years in one of the great fishing-backpacking areas of the country: West Yellowstone, Montana.

Doug McKinsey is familiar with Sierra requirements from his own experience and affiliation with Buz's Fly and Tackle Shop in Visalia, California.

Jim Green is a noted angler, caster and rod designer from Fenwick who combined with Wray Lertora of Fenwick for valuable Pacific Northwest information.

Rex Gerlach has written extensively for newspapers, magazines and books, including *Fly Fishing The Lakes*. Currently he is associated with Daiwa Corporation in Gardena, California.

# 20.

# CAMPFIRE TROUT RECIPES

Freshly caught, cleaned, and prepared trout can provide memorable eating for the backpacking angler. They are delicate and cook quickly, but some caution is advised. Too hot a fire will burn the skin and spoil both the appearance and the flavor; too slow a fire may make them soft. Experienced cooks advise that a cast iron frying pan is ideal. For some forms of car camping and canoe camping this is practical, but the go-light backpacker can make do very well with non-stick lightweight fry pans if attention is paid to the cooking. Also, freshly caught trout may show a tendency to "curl" in the fry pan. If so, a cut into the backbone minimizes or prevents this curling. The needed seasonings can be taken along in little plastic stack packs of the type some fly tying materials come in, or in small plastic bags. Most fried trout recipes are very similar. Here are a few possible variations.

## FRIED TROUT

butter or bacon grease  
salt and pepper to taste  

flour  
lemon juice

Preheat pan over a medium low heat. Apply butter or bacon grease liberally to the pan, but not so much that the trout will be awash. You don't want the grease to enter the body cavity. If using butter, be very careful not to allow the pan to overheat. Butter can scorch easily with excess heat. Dust the trout lightly with flour and a bit of salt and pepper. Lay the fish in and fry equally on each side, about 5 minutes per side, but check by running a knife blade along the dorsal fin and inspect the flesh along the spinal column. When it's flaky, the fish is done. Sprinkle with lemon juice and melted butter.

179

# SCOTCH TROUT VARIATION

Follow recipe as above but roll the trout in oatmeal with a sprinkling of salt and pepper rather than flour.

# CRISPY TROUT

6 small trout
1/3 cup flour or cornmeal
1/2 teaspoon salt

1/2 cup bacon drippings or butter
1 cup granola or chopped almonds
1 tablespoon lemon juice
pepper to taste

Combine flour and seasonings, coat fish, sauté in two batches over medium low heat no more than 5 minutes per side, using half of the fat per batch. Remove fish, then in the same pan, heat granola or chopped almonds, remove from heat, add the lemon juice and pour over fish.

# WHOLE FISH

Prepare a thin paste of equal parts flour and cooking oil. Season to taste with salt and pepper. Coat fish with this mixture, place over medium heat, and cook about 5 minutes per side.

# ALTERNATIVE BATTER

1 cup bisquick
1 egg

salt and pepper to taste
beer

Mix ingredients in bowl, then add enough beer to make a fairly thin batter. Dip fish in the mixture and fry about 5 minutes per side.

# BOILED TROUT

Bring water to a boil with salt and plenty of vinegar in it. Draw the water to the edge of the heat and put in the trout. The water shouldn't boil again. Cook just below the simmering point for about 15 minutes—a bit more or less according to the size of the fish.

Heavy duty aluminum foil is very useful to the backpacking cook. Several variations of foil-wrapped fish are possible. Also, foil can be used to assist in go-light cooking by improvising utensils. With a backpacker's grill, a smooth surface for pan frying can be made by covering the grill with a couple of layers of heavy duty foil wrap. If there is no grill or pan, a forked stick fry pan can be improvised quickly. Secure an appropriate forked stick and mold lengths of heavy duty foil from one side of the fork to the other. Roll up the outer edges of the foil around the "Y" shaped fork to secure them. This leaves a flat center area to hold the food for cooking.

Lacking a forked stick, find a willow switch and loop the narrow end back around to the main stem. The thin tip may be knotted around the main stem or secured with string or "twist 'ems." Leave enough length to serve as a handle. Then mold some heavy duty foil to the circular hoop. Furthermore, a foil saucepan can be made by molding a length of foil around a small stump or log end to your desired size. Leave some excess foil on one side to help form a handle. The foil edges can be folded down to make a rim and the excess foil twisted around a stick to make a suitable handle. A small separate cup to melt margarine or butter can be made by molding the foil around your fist. Remove from your hand and turn down the foil edges.

## GRILLED WHOLE FISH

| | |
|---|---|
| 1 to 3 lb. trout | salt and pepper |
| butter or margarine | 1 medium onion |
| fresh tarragon, parsley, dill, | |
| thyme, rosemary, lemon juice | |

Tear heavy duty foil somewhat longer than the fish, spread butter or margarine in the center of the foil and arrange some onion slices on it. Place the fish on the onion slices. Sprinkle body cavity and outside of the fish with salt and pepper, then top with remaining onion slices and sprinkle with herbs. Bring the foil up and over the fish, sealing all ends with a double fold. Place on grill over medium hot coals. Approximate cooking times: 1 lb. fish in about 15 minutes, a 2 lb. fish in about 25 minutes, and a 3 lb. fish in about 35 minutes. Turn two or three times during the cooking process. Optionally—serve with melted butter to which chopped parsley and lemon juice have been added.

## TROUT AND BACON

Wrap trout in a strip of bacon and lay on foil, cup the foil around the trout. Add juice of a half lemon and thin onion slices, salt and pepper to taste. Fold the foil securely and place in campfire embers. In 10 minutes turn fish. On the average a 12 inch fish will be done in 20 minutes.

## BASIC FOIL TROUT

Lay trout on foil, sprinkle onion in body cavity and over trout. Salt and pepper to taste. Wrap as described above. Cook on rack or in fire embers and serve with melted butter and lemon juice.

# REID'S ARGENTINA VARIATION

Along the charming Calefu in Argentina Douglas Reid prepared a memorable streamside meal. Place trout on foil, arrange sliced onion and tomato in body cavity, salt and pepper to taste. Wrap securely in foil and cook in campfire coals. For a weekend trip or first trail day when weight isn't excessive, serve this variation with wine, cheese, bread and fresh fruit.

*A large brown trout that mistook a deeply drifted Wooly Worm for something more edible.*

# CAMPFIRE TROUT
from Bill Mason

| | |
|---|---|
| Salt and pepper | 4 medium size trout or 2 large trout |
| 1 lemon | grill |
| ½ cup butter or margarine | foil |

Take large fish and filet side; or if smaller trout, split open to lay flat. Salt and pepper. Melt butter or margarine and lemon juice in small pan. Place each trout or filet skin down on hot grill. Baste fish liberally with lemon butter. Repeat periodically. Cover fish with tin foil completely. Let heat from campfire cook the meat portion. Do not turn fish. Cook 5 to 7 minutes or until fish flakes. Serve hot.

# ON THE TRAIL
# BAKED STUFFED BROOK TROUT
from Bob Leeman, Jr.

Stuffing mix
chopped onion and celery
lemon or lemon squeeze

salt and pepper
freshly caught and cleaned brook
 trout

Melt stuffing mix with equal portions of water (amount varies with number of fish prepared). Stir in a sprinkling of chopped onion and celery. Add salt and pepper. Leave the heads on prepared trout to help hold stuffing packed in fish cavities. Wrap in cooking foil and place on edge of hot campfire coals for 10 minutes on each side. Serve with a squeeze of lemon.

# Photo Credits

Page 5, Bill Cairns.
Page 7, Kelty Pack, Inc.
Page 18, Bill Cairns.
Page 21, Kelty Pack, Inc.
Page 23, Eastern Mountain Sports, Inc. 15500 Vose Farm Rd., Peterborough, NH 03458.
Page 24, Jan Sport.
Page 25, Bill Cairns.
Page 29, Diagrams and Boot Construction Information: Courtesy of Recreational Equipment, Inc.
Page 30, Vasque.
Page 33, Bill Cairns.
Page 35, Marmot Mountain Works, Ltd.
Page 36, Jan Sport.
Page 38, Eastern Mountain Sports, Inc.
Page 41, Marmot Mountain Works, Ltd.
Page 44, The Coleman Co., Inc.
Page 47, Eastern Mountain Sports, Inc.
Page 52, Bill Cairns.
Page 55, Orvis Co., Inc.
Page 59, Bill Cairns.
Page 63, Bill Cairns.
Page 64, The Silva Co.
Page 67, 69, 77, 81–85, 87, Bill Cairns.
Page 93, Lefty Kreh.
Page 96, 99, 102, Bill Cairns.
Page 103, Dick Pobst.
Page 106, 107, 109 (top), Bill Cairns.
Page 109 (bottom), Dick Pobst.
Page 111, Bill Cairns.
Page 114, The Orvis Co., Inc.
Page 115–120, 123–125, 127, 128, 132, 133, Bill Cairns.
Page 137, Chart: Courtesy of The Orvis Co., Inc.
Page 138, Toper Charts: Courtesy of the Cortland Line Co.
Page 141, Knot Diagrams: Courtesy of The Orvis Co., Inc.
Page 143, Bill Cairns.
Page 145, The Orvis Co., Inc.
Page 149, Bill Cairns.
Page 150, Cortland Line Co.
Page 154, Bill Cairns.
Page 157, Royal Red Ball.
Page 165, Bill Cairns.
Page 182, Bill Cairns.

# Other Outdoor Books from
# STONE WALL PRESS, INC.

## THE WACKY WORLD OF SKIING
by Craig Peterson and Jerry Emerson

Skiers don't need snow to chuckle at their favorite winter sport! Author Craig Peterson and cartoonist Jerry Emerson have collaborated to produce a unique book of over 100 hilarious cartoons about downhill and cross-country skiing. Emerson's cartoons have appeared in trade journals and major magazines such as the *Saturday Evening Post, Reader's Digest,* and *Parade.* This original collection will delight all skiers. The perfect Christmas gift! 128 pages; 6 × 9. Hardcover, $9.95

## BACKWOODS ETHICS
## Environmental Concerns for Hikers and Campers
Laura & Guy Waterman.

"... undeniably important. They argue that hikers and backpackers must protect natural resources and maintain the 'spirit of wildness' of our country's backwoods ... they describe a new code of backwoods ethics they feel is necessary to accommodate the increasing number of hikers in the wilds."—*PW.* Positive and up-beat, this book documents progress while appealing to a raised natural consciousness. 192 pages. paperback, $6.95

## BACKPACKING FOR TROUT
by Bill Cairns

As the major trout streams become more crowded and less productive, adventuresome fishermen seek out small streams with better opportunities. In this book you will find practical information and advice on how to make your next fishing trip more successful. Planning the trip, the latest in equipment, appropriate technique, and important tips are all carefully discussed and accompanied by the author's illustrations. Illus; Index; 128 pages; 6 × 9. Hardcover, $12.95

## ENJOYING THE ACTIVE LIFE AFTER 50
Ralph H. Hopp.

"An intelligent, informal presentation of the attractions to plus-fifties of out-door activities."—*Kirkus Reviews*. 20 activities are detailed here, and "Hopp's synopsis of each activity is quite personal, studded with stories of his own experiences and discoveries," says *PW*. Foreword by Arthur S. Leon, M.D., Dept. of Medicine, Univ. of Minnesota. Paperback, $6.95


## GOOSE HUNTING
Charles Cadieux

A lifelong waterfowl hunter and outdoor writer artfully interweaves lively, personal stories of goose hunting from Quebec to Mexico with an encyclopedia of facts about good management, good goose hunting and goose watching. With humor and warmth Cadieux covers the controversy about short-stopping, goose calling and its champions, all kinds of decoys, the migration paths of geese, banding, types of geese, and much more. "Anyone else thinking about writing on the subject ought to look at Cadieux's book before star-ting."—*Washington Post*. Hardcover, $14.00


# THE NATURAL WORLD COOKBOOK
## Complete Gourmet Meals from Wild Edibles
by Joe Freitus

At long last we have a complete and comprehensive cookbook of wild, edible foods for the adventuresome gourmet. This is the result of more than fifteen painstaking years of collecting recipes and experi-menting with wild foods. Both plants (Alpine Bilberry to Wintercress) and animals (fish, fowl, and game) are included, along with beautiful line drawings for their easy identification by Salli Haberman.

You will find hundreds of recipes for complete meals that can be prepared from abundant wild foods found across North America. In addition to mouth-watering soup-to-nuts menus, teas, wines and other natural beverages complement each meal. Fare ranges from the usual (Blueberry and Pecan Pies) to the sublime (False Solomon's Seal Soufflé); from the common (Bog Cranberry Bread) to the unique (Woodchuck Pie and Armadillo Stew). Each ingredient is indexed for easy reference. Hardcover, $15.00

# MOVIN' OUT, Equipment & Technique for Hikers
by Harry Roberts

Harry Roberts, ed. of *Wilderness Camping,* updates his solid advice on boots, clothing, packs and sleeping bags, techniques for staying warm, eating well. "An excellent down-to-earth book,"—*International Backpacker Assn.* Illus. Index. Paperback, $4.95 (29-4)

# MOVIN' ON, Equipment & Technique for Winter Hikers

Harry Roberts' companion volume ". . . sets down a lot of good, common-sense advice in an engaging, unpresumptuous style. Roberts' techniques work." *Mountain Gazette.* "A superb book," agrees *Backpacker.* Paperback, $4.95 (23-3)

# WILD PRESERVES,
## Illustrated Recipes for over 100 Natural Jams & Jellies
by Joe Freitus

A comprehensive book on preserving wild fruit. 48 clear illustrations, and over 100 recipes for jams, jellies, pickles, preserves, butter, wine. Paperback, $4.95

# BENEATH THE RISING MIST
by Dana S. Lamb

A Collection of thirty-five pieces by this renowned sportsman and author. "There is a small handful of those today who can write lyrically and yet without pretension about the joys and tragedies the angler or the gunner encounters in the seasons of his year. If there is among this number a more sensitive observer or a more able writer than Dana Lamb, I cannot think who he is."—*Dartmouth Alumni Magazine.* Illus. by Tom Hennessey. Deluxe collector's edition, $15.00 (27-8)

# SKI TOURING in New England and New York—
## A Complete Cross-Country Ski Book.
by Lance Tapley

Lance Tapley brings out the nature and background of x-c skiing in this country, with basic advice on equipment and technique; locates ski-touring areas with details on facilities, outfitters, inns, food, price ranges. Paperback, $4.95 (19-7)

**INTRODUCING YOUR KIDS TO THE OUTDOORS**
by Joan Dorsey

Straightforward advice about outdoor trips with the kids along—carefully planned day hikes proceeding to extended trips; canoeing, bicycling, ski touring. "...she talks about her own rewarding wilderness experiences and all the reasons why children should get outdoors."—*Adventure Travel Newsletter*. Paperback, $4.95 (25-1)

# Books on the Stone Wall Press Backlist

| | |
|---|---|
| Atlantic Surf Fishing, Maine to Maryland *Lester C. Boyd* | $4.95 (P) |
| Bass Fishing in New England *Bob Elliot* | $6.50 (C) |
| Exploring New England Shores,<br>   A Beachcomber's Handbook *Waters* | $7.95 (C) |
| My New England *Frank Woolner* | $10.00 (C) |
| Northeastern Bass Fishing *Bob Elliot* | $4.50 (P) |
| Northeastern Outdoors, A Field & Travel Guide *Steve Berman* | $7.95 (P) |
| 160 Edible Plants, Commonly Found in the US<br>   and Canada *Joe Freitus* | $3.50 (P) |

To order Stone Wall Press books send check or money order to our distributors:

*The Stephen Greene Press*
*Box 1000*
*Brattleboro, VT 05301*